This War Within My Mind
Based on the blog *The Bipolar Battle*

By John Poehler

Dedicated to

The three people who make this life worth living:
Brenna, Emerson, and Annaliese.

Each warrior fighting the daily battle with bipolar disorder.

Robert Allan Payne Jr.
April 28, 1977 ~ November 9, 2009

"Bipolar disorder can dictate your energy level,
your activity level,
even your mood,
but it cannot dictate your willpower."

~ John Poehler

Table of Contents

Foreword.. 13

Preface 15

Introduction.. 19

Suicide 23

   Important Statistics.. 23

   Look for the Warning Signs 23

My Journey to a Diagnosis of Bipolar Disorder 25

Am I in Denial about My Diagnosis?.................................. 31

How Do We Define Our Personal Identity? 35

Create a Treatment Plan and a Crisis Plan........................... 37

   Treatment Plan 37

   Crisis Plan 38

Be Proactive With Your Treatment 41

Advocate for Yourself 43

Bipolar Depression 45

Mania 49

Psychosis 53

   Hallucinations 53

   Delusions.. 55

Hypersexuality... 57

The Impact of High-Risk and Extreme Activities on Bipolar

Disorder... 59

   Extreme Activities.. 59

   Too Much of a Good Thing 59

   High-risk Activities 60

Anxiety 61

Adopt the Mentality of a Warrior..................................... 65

Managing Your Daily Life with Bipolar Disorder 67

   Routine 67

   Prevention Provides Flexibility.................................... 68

Stability, Self-Care, and Coping Strategies 71

   1. Medication Management....................................... 72

2. Therapy...72

3. Exercise and Healthy Eating Choices................................72

4. Sleep 73

5. Treatment of Other Illnesses..74

6. Time with Your Loved Ones 75

7. Aromatherapy and Meditation 75

8. Drinking Water...76

Last Thoughts 76

Classes of Medication 79

Mood Stabilizers...79

Antipsychotics 79

Sleep Aids...80

Antidepressants..80

Stimulants...80

Last Thoughts 81

Weight Gain with Psychotropic Medication 83

Therapy is a Component to Recovery 85

Types of Therapy 85

CBT...85

DBT...85

EMDR..86

Your Support System..87

Find a Support Group 89

In-person Support Group...89

Online Support Group...90

Make Exercise a Priority...91

Consistency is Paramount to a Healthy Lifestyle................94

Balance Should be Your Focus 94

Stop the Black and White Thinking 95

No Crash Diets 95

Electroconvulsive Therapy (ECT) On the Brain 97

What Are Your Expectations? 101

Stigma is Real...103

Common Frustrating Statements...107

People Calling me "Crazy"..107

"We all have a little bipolar in each of us." 107

"It is all in your head." 108

"You have control over this." 108

What Is a Trigger? 111

Types of Triggers Defined 113

1. Stress 113

2. Toxic Relationships 114

3. Death of a Loved One/Bereavement 114

4. Breakup/Divorce 114

5. Sleep 115

6. Seasonal Changes 115

7. Weather Changes 116

8. Alcohol/Drugs 116

9. Pregnancy 117

10. Job Loss 117

10. Medication 117

11. Financial Strain 118

12. Traumatic Event/Victim of a Crime 119

13. Too Much Exercise 119

Last Thoughts 119

Electronic Device Usage 121

Should I Get a Therapy Animal? 123

Money, Money, Money 125

Expenses 126

Income 128

How to Get Energized when You Feel Exhausted and

Depressed 129

1. Get Blood Work 129

2. Create a Routine 130

3. Take a Cat Nap 130

4. Get Outside 130

5. Exercise 131

Last Thoughts 131

Top Careers When You Live With Bipolar Disorder 133

Blog 133

Entrepreneur 134
Freelancer 134
Virtual Assistant 135
Coach 135
Speaker 135
Other Options 136
Should I Tell my Boss I Live With Bipolar Disorder? 136
Last Thoughts 136
Hobbies 139
Art 139
Watching Movies/Television 140
Reading 140
Last Thoughts 140
Long-term and Short-term Goals 141
High Sensitivity and Bipolar Disorder 143
Personal Responsibility 145
Dating and Relationships 147
Parenting When You Have Bipolar Disorder 149
Positive Outcome 149
Negative Consequences 149
How Having Children Affects A Person With Bipolar
Disorder 150
Ways to Get the Most Out of Life 151
1. Follow Your Treatment Plan 151
2. Live a Healthy Lifestyle 151
3. Live Beneath Your Means 152
4. Help Others 152
5. Spend Quality Time with Those You Love 153
6. Find a Hobby 153
Last thought 154
Surviving the Holidays 155
Giving 155
Self-care 155
Moderation 156
Bipolar Disorder is an Illness Men Experience Too 157

Ways to Bounce Back from a Bipolar Episode....................... 161
College... 163
   1. Get Involved 163
   2. Exercise.. 163
                                      3. Sleep 164
   4. Take Some "Me" Time 165
   5. Don't Overextend Yourself... 165
   Last Thoughts... 166
What Is Success when You Live With Bipolar Disorder? 167
Surviving When Your Partner Has Bipolar Disorder 169
   Exercise.. 169
   Self-care 169
   Open Communication.. 170
   Create an Action Plan.. 170
   Last Thoughts 171
Final Thoughts 173
Works Cited 175

Foreword

"I think it's a great way to live, to fight for yourself, to fight for your friends and to fight for a community of individuals who are sharing your experience and who are fighting for their dignity and a better life. In time, there will be a tipping point. Believe me, there will be victories and they will be joyous." ~ Peter Staley

BIPOLAR DISORDER is notoriously hard to describe, but John Poehler finds a way, with delicate empathy to split the mental illness atom with well-researched precision. Bipolar disorder is not an immediately identifiable pain, like that of cancer, a broken bone or a pulled muscle. It may be more accurate to say that despair and hopelessness comes to resemble the diabolical discomfort of being imprisoned in a fiercely overheated room with no way out. And because no breeze stirs this cauldron...it is entirely natural that the victim begins to think ceaselessly of oblivion.

This War Within My Mind is a thoughtful and courageous book written by an up and coming writer who himself has experienced the formidable foe of bipolar I to its maximum persecution. I am tired of hiding, tired of misspent and knotted energies, tired of the hypocrisy, and tired of acting as though I have something to hide. John Poehler's compassionate book shines the necessary light, a disinfectant on what has been for far too long a shameful topic. For too long the first thing people say when I tell them that I'm bipolar is that I should keep quiet about it.

But I've never been good at keeping quiet about anything and John's wonderfully constructed book encourages all of us who suffer, to hold our heads high and speak out with unbridled dignity. We lock arms with confidence that our lives are worth living for.

John's heartfelt work of art, is a must read for all.

Michael J. Whelan
Emmy & Peabody
Award Producer

Preface

MY NAME IS JOHN POEHLER.

I have been educated at the university level earning a B.S. in Natural Sciences with minors in both Math and Chemistry. In addition, I have earned an associate degree in accounting, a certificate in computer specialist, a diploma in sports nutrition and personal training and a CNA certification.

Bipolar Disorder Type 1 is my official diagnosis.

As a disclaimer, I am not a medical professional. I do not have an MD or PhD by my name. Therefore, please be smart when consuming the information contained within the pages of this book. Do not use it to diagnose, cure or treat.

The presented information should not be used as medical advice. Please speak with your doctor if you have a question about a diagnosis or treatment. Remember, you cannot self-diagnosis a mental illness such as bipolar disorder.

Any information used and provided by this book is solely at your own risk.

If you are having a medical crisis, immediately call your doctor, 911 or proceed to your nearest emergency room.

The information that I present here is from my personal experience. I was diagnosed back in 1999 and have 20 years of lived experience fighting in the trenches against bipolar disorder. I have experienced symptoms longer than this as they surfaced before my teenage years.

As someone who has been there, I know what it feels like to live with bipolar disorder and how to successfully manage it with the right treatment and support. I have experienced the paralyzing depths of depression to the psychotic intensity of mania. My hope is that my experience and suggestions will illuminate your own journey.

There are numerous books covering the topic of bipolar disorder, written by doctors, medical professionals and other experts. Many of these publications are wonderful and valuable resources.

As someone who has personal daily experience with bipolar disorder, my hope is to give you a different perspective. I want to share with you what has worked for me to demonstrate that bipolar disorder can be successfully treated.

Let me give you a snapshot from my own journey.

After my initial diagnosis of bipolar disorder, my main focus, and that of my loved ones, was both stabilization and safety. My doctors worked with me to stabilize my mood, both my energy and activity level, and my ability to function. It was my full-time job and I battled for my life.

Since the early years of my diagnosis, I have focused on improving my quality of life. You can use my experience to help you learn about bipolar disorder and how to successfully cope with it.

If you are newly diagnosed with bipolar disorder, then read through these pages to spark ideas about your own treatment. Run them by your doctor to see what they think.

If you are a loved one looking to get information about bipolar disorder, you have come to the right place.

Do not tread lightly on the diagnosis of bipolar disorder. It is a very serious and debilitating illness if not properly treated. I always remember the saying: "it is better to be over-prepared than underprepared."

I know friends and individuals who have lost their lives to the suffocating grip of bipolar disorder. That is why I say not to take your diagnosis lightly.

I created a blog titled *The Bipolar Battle*. You can get more information at: www.thebipolarbattle.com

The mission of *The Bipolar Battle* is "to help empower those living with bipolar disorder live the life they deserve."

The Bipolar Battle has received numerous awards and nominations including:

- Wego Health Award Nomination for "Best in Show: Blog"
- Top 100 Bipolar Disorder Blog
- The Liebster Award
- Blogger Recognition Award
- The Sunshine Blogger Award

I have also been featured on podcasts, radio shows, other websites, nominated for Wego Health Award "Patient Leader Hero", and winner for Wego Health Award "Best in Show: Twitter"

It's empowering to see myself as a warrior, fighter, and survivor. Each day is a battle and I need to make sure I'm in the right frame of mind and have access to the right tools. Only then can I push on to victory.

On that note, let's start learning.

Introduction

BIPOLAR DISORDER is a chronic illness characterized by extreme changes in mood, energy and activity level, motivation and ability to function.

According to the National Institute of Mental Health, bipolar disorder affects about 5.7 million American adults. This is about 2.8 percent of the U.S. population aged 18 and older (Nimh.nih.gov, 2019).

Bipolar type 1 is the so-called textbook version of bipolar disorder as it comes from the original definition of manic depression. The individual cycles from extreme mania down to periods of dark-debilitating depression.

Bipolar type 2 is symptomatically milder compared to bipolar type 1. Individuals with type 2 cycle between hypomania and depression. Hypomania is a milder form of mania. Generally speaking, type 2 does not impact daily functionality to the degree of type 1.

Later in the book, I will go into more detail regarding mania, hypomania, and depression.

Cyclothymic disorder is characterized by brief periods of hypomania alternating with brief periods of depression.

When I speak of mild in relation to the types of bipolar disorder, I mean the symptomology. Bipolar disorder is bipolar disorder no matter which type you are diagnosed. The variability, intensity, and impact of symptoms is greatest in type 1, followed by type 2, and the least with cyclothymic disorder.

There is no conclusive evidence that describes the root cause of bipolar disorder. Studies and research indicate both a genetic and environmental component to bipolar disorder.

Based on current science and research, individuals are genetically predisposed to bipolar disorder. An environmental factor such as an extremely stressful situation or event, generally triggers bipolar disorder and brings it rushing to the surface.

Examples of stress that breach this threshold include any type of trauma, sexual abuse, physical violence, emotional abuse, or a major life change.

A common misconception is that bipolar disorder is only about a simple change in mood. If that was the case, everyone would have bipolar disorder. Also, just because a person has bipolar disorder does not mean they are manic (hypomanic in type 2) or depressed all the time.

In addition to mood variability, individuals with bipolar disorder can yo-yo between staying up for days with an excessive amount of energy to being unable to get out of bed. The variation in energy level is extreme just like the mood variation.

Motivation is generally dictated by energy level. When you have more energy, you are easily motivated. When you can barely lift your head off of your pillow, your energy level is near a non-existent level.

The American Psychiatric Association published a book which outlines the diagnostic criteria for all mental illnesses. The *Diagnostic and Statistical Manual of Mental Disorders*, or DSM, is the doctor's Bible covering officially recognized psychiatric disorders (Diagnostic and Statistical Manual of Mental Disorders, 2017).

The DSM details the different types of bipolar disorder along with their symptoms.

You may have an inclination towards a diagnosis, but discuss it with your doctor. You cannot diagnose yourself.

If you are newly diagnosed with bipolar disorder, I know you have a million questions and a number of mixed emotions. It can be overwhelming to accept that bipolar disorder is a chronic illness. In fact, many people deny their initial diagnosis of bipolar disorder.

When first diagnosed, I felt utter elation. Bipolar disorder was a label to describe my experience. This new discovery proved I was no longer alone. There were others like me.

I felt hope when I learned bipolar disorder is an illness that can successfully be managed with the proper treatment and support. I quickly realized the importance of taking preventative measures to reduce the symptoms and fallout from my newly diagnosed illness.

One of the best ways you can combat denial is through acceptance. The sooner you can accept your diagnosis of bipolar disorder, the faster you can seek out treatment and manage your bipolar disorder.

Another way to combat denial is to educate yourself about your diagnosis. Your newfound knowledge of bipolar disorder will help you discover the best treatment options and best ways to help yourself.

After my original diagnosis, I read as many books as I could get my hands on about bipolar disorder. I read autobiographies to feel that I was not alone. I read books and articles explaining bipolar disorder and what to expect. For the first time, I learned about depression, hypomania, mania and a mixed episode.

I spent weeks reading and educating myself about bipolar disorder and continue to do so to this day. I recommend you do the same.

I hope this book provides a diving board into the water of your lifelong journey of learning.

You will need to make adjustments in your life, but you have to do that with any adversity you experience. Take a proactive role in the treatment and management of your illness. Don't become another victim.

Never give up hope. There is light at the end of the tunnel.

A large portion of my time is focused on managing my bipolar disorder. Luckily, many of the techniques I use in one area of my life branches out into the others.

Notice the different approaches, techniques and ideas I describe in the following pages.

Whether you are newly diagnosed or a seasoned veteran, you are a bipolar warrior in the daily fight against *The Bipolar Battle.*

Suicide

SUICIDE IS VERY REAL.
> It does not discriminate.
> It is an equal opportunity killer.
> Everyone is impacted by suicide, whether directly or indirectly. Whether you live with bipolar disorder or not, suicide affects lives.

If you or someone you know is thinking about suicide or death, call the Lifeline (USA) at 1-800-273-8255. You can also text SIGNS to 741741, 24/7/365 for anonymous free crisis counseling. If you are concerned about someone's immediate safety, call 911 or get them to your nearest Emergency Room.

Important Statistics
According to the American Foundation for Suicide Prevention:
- Each year 44,965 Americans die by suicide
- For every successful suicide, around 25 attempt
- Suicide is the 10th leading cause of death in the United States
- Costs associated with suicide cost the U.S. close to $69 billion annually
- Men die by suicide 3.53 times more than women
- In 2016, firearms accounted for 51 percent of all suicides

These numbers and statistics show just how much of an epidemic suicide has become (AFSP, 2019).

Look for the Warning Signs
- Excessive or too little sleep
- Obsessing about death
- Getting affairs in order
- Withdrawing

- Increase in alcohol or drug use
- Talking about suicide
- Discussing being a burden on others
- Exhibiting feelings of hopelessness or no purpose
- Talking about feeling trapped or in extreme pain

This isn't an exhaustive list of warning signs. Every person is different.

If you experience thoughts of suicide or any of the warning signs, reach out to someone. Preferably, a medical professional. If you decide to confide in another person, make sure you feel comfortable and trust the individual.

Just like bipolar disorder, one of the best ways to fight the stigma of suicide is to talk about it. Educate yourself and those around you.

Let others know that you are there for them.

My Journey to a Diagnosis of Bipolar Disorder

I WAS DIAGNOSED at the end of the summer of 1999.

I have always felt different in some way, I just could never put my finger on it. It actually started in my early teens and I immediately sought out the counsel of adults. I was told that all teenagers experience self-doubt and not to worry.

This did not alleviate my worry and self-doubt.

Back in 1992, the upper left lobe of my lung was surgically removed. At the time, I had many questions and was unsure how to deal with them.

I used my religious upbringing as a way to cope with the situation.

Before my operation, I prayed to God to take my life during my surgery. These were my first thoughts of suicide. Before now, I never told anybody about those thoughts.

Around the same time, I felt extreme sadness for no reason. I had no energy to do anything.

One of my best friends told me I was boring and didn't want to hang out anymore. I remember him telling me I never wanted to do anything. That broke my heart.

I felt flawed. I felt like an outcast.

Looking back, I was depressed. My friend didn't care. I attended a religious private school that neither believed in nor instructed its students on the topic of mental illness or mental health.

As the years went by, my mood swings increased in intensity. I felt either depressed or irritated and angry. My energy level and motivation both waxed and waned. I became an expert in covering up my emotions. I became the "smiling" guy.

I reminded myself what the adults explained to me before: *all teenagers experience self-doubt and not to worry*. This was "normal." This reminder did not help me.

The summer before my junior year in high school, I visited my dad out in Colorado. I worked at a youth employment agency sponsored by the local YMCA.

I met a lovely and attractive young woman during one of the jobs. She was sunbathing on her back porch while I worked in the backyard. For the handful of days I worked at her place, she always initiated conversation. I remember her telling me I should move out to Colorado. She explained there was a "countless supply of hotties like me"- her own words - living in Colorado.

My desire had been to live with my dad and finish high school. The opportunity this woman presented to me sealed the deal. I never spoke to her again, but she was instrumental in helping me take action.

In the fall of 1996, I started my junior year in high school. At the time, my dad and stepmom lived in Boulder.

I enjoyed those last couple years of high school tremendously. I made some amazing friends that I still speak to today. I was also elected senior class president. Looking back, this is when my bipolar disorder began to intensify and make a name for itself.

During those last couple of years living with my dad and stepmom, I bounced from hypomania and plummeted back down to depression. Extreme irritability consumed me. My mood would change with the flick of a switch. My stepmom recently told me that she never knew what to expect when I came home.

My friends used to say, "I want whatever you are on." At the time, my energy level was over the top and I could hardly contain it.

I took some classes on how to lift weights and lifting became my daily therapy. Weight lifting was my primary outlet and coping strategy. I channeled my extra energy through lifting weights and I loved it.

In 1998, I graduated from high school and moved up to Fort Collins, Colorado. I began my college experience at Colorado State University. My focus of study was chemical engineering.

The first semester I lived in a dorm. At the end of that semester I had a serious altercation with my roommate. As a result, I moved to another dorm and roomed with one of my good high school buddies.

One night, at the beginning of my second semester, I drank too much alcohol while speaking to a close friend on the phone. I don't remember specifics to the conversation but I know my friend was concerned.

A police officer came barging into my dorm room in the middle of the night. He explained someone (my close friend) called and was concerned for my well-being and worried about my safety. I was upset, but I assured the officer I would be fine. There was no cause for concern. With that, he left.

The next day my RA contacted me and explained the counseling center wanted to speak with me. The counseling center received information regarding the incident of the previous night. I refused at first, but quickly changed my mind. I realized this could possibly help me to find some answers as to why I have always dealt with things differently, compared to my peers.

For the next few months, I spoke with countless medical professionals and went through rigorous testing. My diagnosis switched through various psychiatric conditions.

Specifically, I remember cyclothymia, ADHD and schizoaffective disorder. I received my answer before the start of my sophomore year in college.

During the summer, one of my new college buddies and I roomed together. We enrolled in summer classes at Colorado State University.

This is when bipolar disorder fully unveiled its ugly face.

I started to hallucinate and become delusional, but I didn't know it at the time. My need for sleep was nonexistent. I worked out twice a day and still had plenty of energy to spare.

I didn't know what was happening. My mind was traveling in a dozen different directions. The line between reality and fiction morphed together.

Luckily, during this chaotic and psychotic time, I saw an amazing psychiatrist through the CSU health center. She was literally my salvation.

She looked at my history and background through my medical records. I sat there with my newly bleached hair and tongue piercing. After an extensive and lengthy discussion, she said I had a clear case of bipolar disorder. This was my initial diagnosis.

Immediately, she treated me with an arsenal of potent psychotropic medications and I was hospitalized. Afterwards, I quickly came crashing down.

Over the next couple years, I saw close to 10 doctors that each independently diagnosed me with bipolar disorder type 1. I even flew out to California to participate in an experimental brain scan. The brain scan provided support to my diagnosis of bipolar disorder.

There was no doubt in my mind: I had bipolar disorder type 1.

I felt like a guinea pig seeing so many doctors, going through various procedures, and exploring ways to manage my bipolar disorder. Throughout the process, I maintained persistence and did not give up. It took my desire and willingness to find answers to discover my diagnosis of bipolar disorder.

If you have not been diagnosed or are newly diagnosed with bipolar disorder, I suggest you take action. Strive to become an expert in the symptomatology of your own bipolar disorder. Educate yourself and seek answers; don't sit and wait for them to find you.

Become your own best advocate. After all, medication, treatment and theories about bipolar disorder are constantly changing.

Am I in Denial about My Diagnosis?

COMPARED TO MOST PEOPLE, I had a different reaction to my initial diagnosis of bipolar disorder type 1.

Most people have mixed emotions when they are newly diagnosed. You find out not only that you have a mental illness, but you will have to manage bipolar disorder for the rest of your life.

It can be pretty frightening.

I began questioning my reason for existence as early as 6 or 7 years old. I was just a kid, but I remember those intense feelings, thoughts and images within my mind.

I felt connected to the world in a special way. Not the type of special your parents explain you are to them.

I believed that somehow, my presence on Earth contributed to the intricate fabric and natural order of the world around me. I just didn't know how.

Around the time I was 12 years old, I learned that the upper left portion of my lung was nonfunctioning. Luckily, I learned of this scary fact after I collided with a classmate during a friendly game of tag. Otherwise, you may not be reading these words right now.

The collision with my friend felt like divine intervention.

I attended a small private Christian Science school in Saint Louis, Missouri. A visit to a doctor was an exception, not a rule.

After the collision with my friend, my breathing became more labored as the days went by. My late grandfather helped me get to a hospital. It was right after the end of my sixth grade year in elementary school.

I needed surgery to remove the diseased and dead part of my lung. The revelation of my lung sparked thoughts and feelings I did not understand.

If I was put on this planet for something special, why would God take me so early in my life?

My spiritual connection with the world seemed so supernatural and real. This situation didn't make sense to me.

I remember having a discussion with God.

God and I spoke to one another like friends on the street. This conversation took place in my mind but was real as the air you breathe. I asked Him to take me from this life if I was not put on this Earth to do something special. In my mind, what was the point of my life if I didn't have some integral divine purpose in the world?

"Please, if I'm not here to do something special, let me fall asleep with the anesthesia and do not allow me to wake up. If you have other plans for me, please wake me up when I am done with surgery."

After my surgery, I woke up in recovery. I now had the answer to my question.

From my perspective, I was alive and God made it so. Every time a doctor or nurse came in to check on me or perform a procedure, I thanked them profusely. Over and over. I was beyond grateful to God and I wanted to spread gratitude to those around me.

What was to be my special role in this world?

With my divinely instilled purpose, I began questioning and searching.

My diagnosis of bipolar type 1 provided me an answer. I felt such relief. There are so many tools and options to treat bipolar, function to the best of your ability, and improve your quality of life.

Many feel defeated and discouraged to learn of their diagnosis. We use labels for pretty much everything. The term "mental illness" or "bipolar disorder" is not well received by others. There is a HUGE stigma associated with these terms.

Since I was first diagnosed back in 1999, we as a society have come so far in educating the general public about bipolar disorder. There is hope in reducing the stigma surrounding bipolar disorder. There is still a long way to go but we are taking steps forward. This is progress.

After you are newly diagnosed, it is normal to react with feelings of denial. Accept your diagnosis as soon as you are able to feel comfortable. Then move on. Otherwise, you will stay in a holding pattern and unable to get better. Ultimately, bitterness and anger will take hold. Without proper treatment, you will more than likely get worse.

One of the ways you can accept your diagnosis is by taking action. It is quite empowering to take healthy action.

You can empower yourself by:
- Reading books about bipolar disorder
- Researching your new diagnosis
- Creating a treatment plan with your doctor and loved ones
- Putting together a crisis plan with your doctor and loved ones
- Seeing a doctor on a regular basis
- Making an ongoing appointment with a therapist

These are ways to take charge of bipolar disorder.

Once you are able to accept your diagnosis of bipolar disorder, you'll be able to move forward. I am not saying this is an easy task. It takes work but is realistic and in your power.

How Do We Define Our Personal Identity?

PERSONAL IDENTITY IS DEFINED AS "The concept you develop about yourself that evolves over the course of your life. This may include aspects of your life that you have no control over, such as where you grew up or the color of your skin, and the choices you make in life, such as how you spend your time and what you believe (Study.com, 2019)."

Bipolar disorder falls in line with, "may include aspects of your life that you have no control over." It is easy to feel like you have no control living with bipolar disorder. I've been there and completely understand.

It isn't a stretch to identify as bipolar disorder. It is difficult to distinguish between yourself and your illness. Each person exhibits varying intensity of symptoms.

To help understand your own bipolar disorder, write in a mood journal to record your mood, energy level, motivation, and both your feelings and reactions to situations. This will help you to distinguish between your bipolar disorder and yourself. It will also provide you a tool to learn your own symptomology between the two poles of depression and mania (hypomania with bipolar type 2).

How you describe yourself will impact your personal identity.

Instead of saying *I am bipolar*, I say, *I have bipolar* or *I live with bipolar disorder*. Do you see the distinction? The first statement indicates that bipolar is your sole identity. The second statement suggests that bipolar is separate from yourself. This subtle clarification can help you understand and articulate your own personal identity. Words have more power than you may realize.

You are not exclusively defined by bipolar disorder. It has a direct influence on who you are as a person but it is not your only defining characteristic.

Someone who has diabetes is not defined solely by diabetes. They simply live with it, and it is something to manage. The same goes for bipolar disorder.

Determining where bipolar disorder ends and your personality begins is difficult but doable. After all, it affects every part of your life and is all-consuming.

When I am in a stable state, I like to do some serious introspection. I have the opportunity to ask, "Who am I?" It gives me a chance to reflect on how much control I do have and to focus on managing my illness.

Over the many years of dealing with bipolar disorder I have learned what makes me tick; the things that are important to me. This is how I have defined my personal identity.

I see myself as a warrior fighting this battle, The Bipolar Battle. This perspective provides me hope that I can fight this illness and manage it.

You can't figure out who you really are while manic or depressed. These are episodic states that come and go. Mania and depression are components to bipolar disorder. You cannot realistically define anything in either of these states of mind.

You are a person and human being first and foremost. Bipolar disorder directly impacts who you are as a person, but it does not define you.

Create a Treatment Plan and a Crisis Plan

WHEN IT COMES TO creating a plan to help manage your illness, do not get caught up in semantics. You can name it anything you want. I just happen to call it a treatment plan and a crisis plan. You can call it whatever you want.

It is a good idea to create each plan with your doctor along with input from your loved ones. When everything is said and done, make sure to give a copy to your doctor and pass it on to those in your support network.

Treatment Plan

A treatment plan is your daily plan of attack to manage your bipolar disorder. Write down what you would like to accomplish each day and during a week (7 days). Each plan is different, and you can mold it to your own personal liking.

Your treatment plan is comprised of medication management, homeopathic approaches, coping strategies and self-care activities such as therapy, exercise and meditation. The specifics to each of these components should be written down.

I have a list of non-negotiables I need to get done every day, no exceptions. These are things that cannot be put off until tomorrow.

My daily non-negotiables include taking my medications in the morning and night. I also exercise each day, get outside regardless of the weather, and get at least 8 hours of sleep.

My weekly task includes writing my blog. I do not like to schedule my writing. So, I just make sure that I write a few days each week to complete my weekly blog posts.

The non-negotiables are the bare minimum I need to complete. I also include other activities that I'd like to complete each day as well.

When I first created my treatment plan, I listed my various activities in a column along with corresponding boxes to the right of each activity. At the top of the column above the activity boxes, I wrote the date for that particular day. As I completed each task, I put an "x" in the corresponding completed box.

I no longer "x" out my tasks because it is pretty ingrained in my head what I need to accomplish each day. I know what needs to be done between the time my head lifts off the pillow and I lay down to sleep each night.

Some people like to list their current medications on their treatment plan.

Like I said above, each treatment plan is unique to each person. Include sections and activities that will help you. It is for your personal benefit and to foster a sense of control in your life.

Crisis Plan

Implement your crisis plan when in crisis. Here a crisis is a manic or depressive episode.

Think about these questions when creating your crisis plan:

What action should I take if I get manic or depressed?

What actions should my loved ones take if I get manic or depressed?

Is there anybody I can specifically call in a crisis?

Where should I go in case of an emergency?

Even if you do not write something down, please talk to your doctor and the rest of your support team. Explain what you want them to do if you start struggling. For instance, what steps should your doctor take if you start to sink into a depressive state or jump into a manic episode?

This plan should have a list of those you want to call in case of crisis, along with their phone numbers. Generally, you will have your doctor first, your therapist second, and other support members after that.

You should have two different sections below your contacts. One title should read **Depressive Episode** and the other **Manic Episode**.

In each section, write how you would like your mental health care team to treat you and when they should get you to a hospital. Write down the steps your healthcare team should take in case of a crisis.

Not everyone is compliant when they experience an episode. If this is you, you should express this concern to your healthcare team so they can take the proper steps to support you.

Some individuals take preparatory legal action. A lawyer can draw up the proper documents to switch your decision making responsibility to a loved one in case you get extremely sick. This is a good option if you are married, in a serious-committed relationship, and/or have children in the picture. Decision making responsibility would switch back once your doctor gives their medical ok saying you are healthy.

The best way to follow this legal route is to speak to a lawyer or find a do-it-yourself website to walk you through the appropriate steps.

Please note this is not legal advice and should not be taken that way. Always speak with a lawyer if you have questions.

Creating a treatment plan and a crisis plan is a positive and proactive approach. Both plans detail preventative measures and provide a plan of attack to manage your bipolar disorder.

Following your treatment plan is a way to take positive action. Follow your treatment plan each day.

Remember, by empowering yourself in healthy ways, you increase your chances of success in living a full and productive life.

Be Proactive With Your Treatment

THE BEST WAY TO MANAGE bipolar disorder is to take a proactive approach. This will give you back some control and is extremely empowering.

Following my treatment plan is a way I take healthy action every day. It is imperative that I take action no matter how much energy I can afford for that particular day.

Something is always better than nothing. If you only have enough energy to roll out of bed, brush your teeth, and then lay back down, so be it. That is still action. You are doing the best you can, with what you have, at the time. Do your best not to beat yourself up over it.

Your energy level and motivation can change from day to day. Be honest with yourself regarding your ability to conquer a certain task. Don't excuse inaction if you have the energy and motivation to do something.

I view my daily fight with bipolar disorder as "The Bipolar Battle" because of the continual onslaught of change.

What do you think of when I say battle?

I think of warriors.

Warriors do not let the world dictate their lives. They make things happen.

With bipolar disorder, you are constantly at the whim of your biology. You can't will yourself to feel a certain way.

How are you supposed to look at yourself as a warrior, who makes things happen, when your bipolar disorder maintains so much control?

The answer is to take preventative measures. You do this by following your treatment plan and crisis plan.

Taking a proactive approach to your treatment will give you back some control over a serious and debilitating mental illness.

Advocate for Yourself

YOU CAN ADVOCATE FOR YOURSELF by reading books, articles, and studies about bipolar disorder. With the knowledge, you will have a better ability to voice your thoughts, ideas, and concerns to the medical professional overseeing your treatment.

You are your own best advocate.

A doctor will monitor and dispense your medication. Most patients see their medical professional on a monthly basis. These appointments can increase or decrease based on the symptomatology of your illness.

When you go in for an appointment, have your questions written down in a notebook. Optimize the time with your doctor by having these questions ready ahead of time. If you write in a mood journal, make sure to bring that as well. Most of these medical professionals have very limited time in their schedules.

Always remember that doctors are only human. Sometimes relaying information to their patients is overlooked.

Medication is a perfect example. If you are prescribed a new medication, ask questions such as:

What are the side effects?

How is this supposed to help me?

When should I take it?

How long until it becomes therapeutic in my system?

No question is a dumb one. If you do not like the answer to one of your questions, discuss it with your doctor.

Don't just take your script for a medication and leave your appointment. Ask questions, so you know what you are getting yourself into.

The whole process of managing your illness is a daunting one. Especially when you are first diagnosed. It is overwhelming. These uneasy feelings will dissipate over time.

You will feel better when you take control of what you can.

Create and follow your treatment plan and crisis plan. Contributing to your treatment plan and crisis plan will give you back control. It will also help you to manage bipolar disorder.

If you have a question, ask it.

If you have an idea, share it.

The medical professional you are working with is your ally and not your enemy. Start advocating for yourself and become your own best advocate.

Bipolar Depression

SYMPTOMS OF DEPRESSION include (Healthline, 2019):
- Changes in appetite or weight, sleep, or psychomotor activity
- Decreased energy
- Feelings of worthlessness or guilt
- Trouble thinking, concentrating, or making decisions
- Thoughts of death or suicidal plans or attempts
- Increased negative self-talk

If you or someone you know is thinking about death or suicide, call the Suicide Prevention Hotline at 800-273-8255. You can also call 9-1-1 or get to your nearest emergency room.

Bipolar depression is different compared to unipolar depression. Because they are different, the treatment plan for bipolar depression is unlike that of unipolar depression.

Suffering from bipolar depression feels like your body is shutting down. It affects your entire being, both mind and body.

Your thoughts slow down to a crawl, and it's hard to focus and comprehend those around you. Upon waking, your body feels achy. Sometimes it feels like you have a cold or respiratory infection when in fact, you do not.

The first therapist I saw called my thoughts *stinkin' thinkin'* while I was in the throes of bipolar depression.

Thoughts of hopelessness filled my mind. I felt stuck in a corner and unable to move. There was no light at the end of the tunnel; I felt like nothing in my life would get better or improve.

I found fault in every part of my life. My mind tricked me into second guessing all of my thoughts, actions, and decisions.

Every decision I made, I found a flaw. In fact, I could no longer make decisions. They were too daunting.

Life was too overwhelming to live.

My body slowed down and my ability to do anything was nonexistent.

I remember seeing a commercial of a swimming pool filled with caramel. Two people were in it trying to run. They tried to move, but they could not. This is a metaphor of bipolar depression when you try to move. You try to function but you simply cannot.

Being around others is not an option. It is something you cannot handle.

With bipolar depression, you will oversleep or under sleep. Personally, I oversleep. I can barely get out of bed, if at all. Others can hardly sleep. It is similar to insomnia.

In extreme cases of bipolar depression, thoughts of suicide will enter your mind. This generally comes at a point when you feel too much pain and do not want to suffer from it any longer. Overwhelming thoughts of doom take over. Hopelessness becomes all-consuming.

Do not let yourself reach this hopeless point. Reach out to someone you trust. Everybody needs extra support at some point. Remember, reaching out for help is never a sign of weakness; it is a sign of strength to accept where you are and to take action.

Your crisis plan needs to state what your doctor and loved ones should do in case you experience a depressive episode.

You may be wondering what kind of treatment exists for bipolar depression.

New medications are coming on the market that are specifically designed for bipolar depression.

Antidepressants are an option, but not many doctors will prescribe an antidepressant to someone with bipolar disorder type 1. If you are taking mood stabilizers and/or antipsychotics, your doctor may consider antidepressants. The downside is they can take four to six weeks to work.

There are some new options that work faster and provide quicker relief than antidepressants.

Speak with your doctor and research your options. Your doctor will ultimately have the final say, but make sure you feel comfortable with their decision and that your voice is heard.

Bipolar disorder is an illness, and you did not choose to feel this way. The symptoms you experience while in a depressive episode are not character flaws.

Mania

SYMPTOMS OF MANIA include (Eveningpsychiatrist.com, 2019):

- Inflated self-esteem or grandiosity
- Decreased need for sleep (e.g. you feel rested after only 3 hours of sleep)
- More talkative than usual or pressure to keep talking
- Insomnia or hypersomnia nearly every day
- Psychomotor agitation (observable by others, not merely subjective feelings of restlessness or being slowed down)
- Flight of ideas or subjective experience that thoughts are racing
- Distractibility (i.e., attention too easily drawn to unimportant or irrelevant external stimuli)
- Increase in goal-directed activity (either socially, at work, at school, or sexually)
- Excessive involvement in pleasurable activities that have a high potential for painful consequences (e.g., engaging in unrestrained buying sprees, sexual indiscretions, or foolish business investments)

Most people perceive that going through a manic episode is this great and wonderful thing. Generally, the so-called fun part of mania is short lived.

Do not mess around with mania, it is more intense and problematic than people portray it to be.

When I experience a manic episode, the first few days are like heaven. It feels like I am wrapped up in joy. I require little to no amount of sleep. Wonderful, creative, and innovative ideas flow through my head. I have extra energy to clean and work on my new ideas, and I have an inclination to make friends in a heartbeat.

I feel euphoric.

It is evident when the euphoric part of my mania ends, and things begin to change. Irritability sets in, and I am easily annoyed. Hallucinations and delusions show their ugly faces. With psychosis, you cannot work on your projects and ideas. The extra energy is not channeled towards cleaning or other positive outlets.

Everyone who lives with bipolar disorder does not necessarily experience psychosis. The ones who do are diagnosed with bipolar disorder type 1. Even then, not everybody with bipolar disorder type 1 experiences hallucinations and delusions. This is an example of being diagnosed with the same mental illness but exhibiting different symptoms.

Doctors try their best to reduce the intensity of a manic episode. After all, what goes up must come down. The higher the way up, the greater the fall.

The opposite pole to mania is bipolar depression. The more extreme the manic episode, the greater the intensity of the depressive episode. The greater the strength of the manic episode, the longer it takes to recover. For the majority, bipolar depression follows a manic episode.

Medication helps to reduce the severity of mania and sometimes eliminate it altogether. I for one, need to be on medication. Otherwise, I can go right into a manic tailspin.

One of the symptoms of mania is poor decision making. Examples include having unprotected sex with a number of different partners, driving a car to extreme and erratic speeds, spending money frivolously, and even uprooting and moving to another country or place. Many individuals living with bipolar disorder have been incarcerated as a result of their poor decision making.

I have never been one to use my illness as a scapegoat for my personal behavior. I take many preventative measures to manage my bipolar disorder, and this has reduced the negative fallout from my manic episodes.

I still experience manic episodes, don't get me wrong, but they are not as frequent. The repercussions are lessened because I stay on my medication under the supervision of my doctor.

The greater the strength of the manic episode, the longer it takes to recover.

Mania is not all fun and games. People can get hurt. Lives can be ruined.

Put a plan in place to protect yourself and loved ones. This would be a great opportunity to create your treatment plan and crisis plan if you have not done so already.

Psychosis

THE DICTIONARY DEFINES PSYCHOSIS as, "a severe mental disorder in which thought and emotions are so impaired that contact is lost with external reality (Lexico Dictionaries | English, 2019)."

There are two main components to psychosis: delusions and hallucinations.

Everyone that has bipolar disorder does not necessarily experience psychosis. Those with bipolar disorder type 1 can experience psychosis and even then, not all patients do.

I have experienced both delusions and hallucinations firsthand.

Let us take a further look at hallucinations.

Hallucinations

The dictionary defines a hallucination as, "an experience involving the apparent perception of something not present (Lexico Dictionaries | English, 2019)."

In other words, you experience something that is not really there with one or more of your five senses. The types of hallucinations include auditory, olfactory, tactile, gustatory, kinesthetic, or visual.

Auditory: Hear sounds and noises that are not real.

Olfactory: Smell an aroma or odor that is not present.

Tactile: Feel something crawl all over your body when there is nothing there. Some individuals feel pressure like someone is touching them. Others feel the sensation of water hitting their skin.

Gustatory (Taste): Have a strong taste that is not there. For example, some individuals may have a metallic taste in their mouth that is not the result of a physical ailment.

Kinesthetic: Think your body is in motion when it is not. For example, flying, walking, running, or falling.
Visual: See shapes, colors, objects, or people that are not there.

Those living with bipolar disorder type 1 are more likely to have auditory hallucinations as opposed to visual hallucinations.

Hallucinations have been a hallmark symptom of mine while living through a manic episode. Examples of my auditory hallucinations include music and static from a radio station without listening to an actual radio. I have heard a voice shouting my name over and over; the voice commanded me to hurt myself. I later learned there was no radio nor person around. It was all a part of my bipolar disorder.

My visual hallucinations include dark human-like figures, demon-like figures, the walls moving, insects crawling in and out of my arms and hands, black blobs floating in front of me, and colorful auras flickering. Again, these were not really there.

I have also experienced tactile hallucinations. I have felt rushing water all over my body. No one was pouring water over me, and I wasn't taking a shower.

I experience psychosis while manic or in a mixed episode. I have never experienced psychosis while depressed.

Since my last manic episode, I have heard static from a radio. This is my first experience, since being diagnosed, of having a hallucination without mania. It has not affected my daily living, so with the advice of my doctor I just monitor it to make sure things do not adversely impact my functionality.

Hopefully this gives you a better idea regarding hallucinations.

Now, let us continue our discussion with delusions.

Delusions

The dictionary defines a delusion as, "an idiosyncratic belief or impression that is firmly maintained despite being contradicted by what is generally accepted as reality or rational argument, typically a symptom of a mental disorder (Lexico Dictionaries | English, 2019)."

A delusion is similar to a hallucination in that an individual believes in something that is not really taking place in reality.

The best way to further define a delusion is to give you an example from my own life.

Back in 2015, I had a faith-based delusion. I felt I was best friends with the Pope both in my heart and mind. Together, I felt that the Pope and I could revolutionize all of Christianity for the better. In fact, I thought I could easily get the Pope on the phone to discuss this further; I even considered travelling to the Vatican in order to speak with him in person. My friendship with the Pope was not rational or based in reality, but it was as real to me as the air you breathe.

During a separate manic episode, the devil and his legions of fallen angels were coming for my family, myself included. I possessed the spiritual power and enlightenment to protect them.

These are not rational beliefs.

Psychosis is very real and has played a major role in my bipolar disorder. It can be extremely scary. Luckily, I have a wonderful support system to help keep me in check.

If psychosis is part of your symptomatology, add it to your crisis plan. Enlist the help of your loved ones, and make sure to have a backup plan in place. This way, you can protect yourself and those around you.

Hypersexuality

SEX IS A TOPIC that many people feel uncomfortable talking about. Growing up many of our parents didn't speak about sex. Whatever the reason, sex has been a taboo topic since day one.

Most of us diagnosed with bipolar type 1 can relate to hypersexuality. A person's innate desire for sexual contact shoots through the roof. Sex becomes all consuming, almost to the point of obsession.

Let's take an example. A stable individual may be sexually satisfied after engaging in one sexual act a week with their partner.

Now, this same person is thrown into a manic episode. Their need for sexual contact increases to multiple times a day.

With hypersexuality, sex is not just a simple desire. Sex acts like a drug. The manic individual becomes obsessed with sex and has tunnel vision for it.

The frequency of sex isn't the only thing that changes during a manic episode. The morals and values of this individual can take a 180 degree turn.

Another example would be during a period of stability, a particular individual is extremely conservative and monogamous. During a manic episode, hypersexuality takes over.

This person's conservative and monogamous values abruptly change. What was once seen as off limits in the bedroom, seems perfectly acceptable. This individual seeks out multiple partners and experiments in new sexual ways. There are no longer a set of values and morals.

The perspective and thoughts of an individual during mania becomes extremely skewed.

Bipolar disorder is an illness and not a decision. However, this doesn't give you a free pass to do what you want without consequence. This solidifies the importance of taking preventative measures before something detrimental occurs in your life.

Communication is key.

If you are in a relationship, it is imperative that you discuss your hypersexuality with your partner. You need to be completely honest with your changing desires and needs.

Again, each person is different when it comes to their own symptomatology. Everybody doesn't experience hypersexuality.

If hypersexuality is a part of your bipolar disorder, have a frank and open conversation with your partner.

What are your symptoms during mania?

Make sure to set up roadblocks and contingencies.

Find ways to reduce the manic fallout from an episode. The consequences can be disastrous and kill a perfectly sound relationship if you don't take preventative action.

Bipolar disorder is such an inconsistent illness. There are surprises all the time. You need to be proactive and do what you can to prevent these surprises.

Everyone doesn't experience the same intensity and change in sexual desire during a manic episode.

Don't allow the consequences of hypersexuality to take you by surprise.

The Impact of High-Risk and Extreme Activities on Bipolar Disorder

BIPOLAR DISORDER IS AN ILLNESS of chaos. You can expect extreme changes in mood, energy level, and motivation. Bipolar disorder can also negatively impact your focus and attention. These shifts can wreak havoc in your life if you don't take the proper precautions.

Again, maintaining moderation and balance in your daily life will help to foster long-term stability.

Extreme Activities

Extreme activities and experiences can result in the destabilization of your bipolar disorder.

Have you ever participated in an extreme sport?

Examples of extreme sports include skydiving, rock climbing, motor cross, bungee jumping, and speed racing.

We already know that stress is a trigger of a mood episode. It makes sense that a spike in your adrenaline can trigger an episode.

Extreme sports are not the only activities that can pump up your adrenaline. Any type of stressful situation can increase your adrenaline.

The likelihood of an episode increases as the length of time of the extreme activity gets greater and greater. Please keep this in mind as you participate in any events or activities.

I'm not saying you should stop participating in life. Just be cautious when putting your long-term stability at risk.

Ask yourself this question: *Is it worth it?*

Too Much of a Good Thing

Overdoing anything can trigger a mood episode. Too much of a good thing can actually be detrimental to your health.

Along with the other aspects of your life, practice moderation.

As you know by now, bipolar disorder is an illness of extremes. As an illness of extremes, it is logical that participating in an extreme activity can trigger a manic episode.

If you are ever unsure about a particular activity, the best way to tackle your uncertainty is to pull back the reins. Start slowly and don't overdo it. It is better to utilize caution than to trigger an episode and deal with the negative fallout. You won't be able to function if you fly into a manic episode or crash into a depressive episode.

Stability is my number one goal. Stability allows me to be the best husband and father I can be. If that means that I need to take a step back or slow down, so be it.

Make a healthy lifestyle a requirement in your long-term treatment plan.

High-risk Activities

High-risk activities are generally symptomatic of bipolar disorder.

There are a number of high-risk activities doctors use to help identify a mood episode.

For example, frivolous overspending is a hallmark of bipolar disorder. That being said, everyone who is diagnosed with bipolar disorder does not necessarily exhibit this behavior.

The same can be said for hypersexuality.

Remember, everyone presents differently when it comes to their bipolar disorder.

Anxiety

ANXIETY IS A COMMON SYMPTOM of bipolar disorder.

Everyone experiences anxiety to some degree. It is part of our natural survival instinct. That feeling of fight or flight helps to protect us. However, things become problematic when you become trapped in fight or flight mode.

A neurotypical individual (someone without a mental illness) reacts to anxiety by choosing to take flight and run or stay and fight. The mind of a person living with bipolar disorder functions differently than that of a neurotypical person.

A seemingly normal situation can trigger anxiety or panic to an epic level in a person living with bipolar disorder.

Most of the time your anxiety will go away with the proper treatment of your illness, but this is not always the case.

I took anti-anxiety medication for several years. As time crept by I realized, with the help of my doctor and therapist, this medication merely masked my anxiety. It did not allow me to properly fight this particular part of my battle.

I utilized a different approach. I focused on dealing with my feelings during a panic or anxiety attack. Like the other aspects of my treatment, I shifted my perspective towards prevention. I did this by working with my therapist and weaning off my anti-anxiety medication under the supervision of my doctor.

You will not always find immediate results when working on prevention. Prevention is a culmination of daily activities, rituals and coping techniques.

Try some of these suggestions and see what works for you:
1. Meditate
2. Exercise
3. Reframe Your Thoughts/Perspective
4. Aromatherapy

5. Warm Bath or Shower
6. Deep Breathing
7. Abdominal Breathing
8. Get at Least 8 Hours of Sleep
9. Make Healthy Eating Choices
10. Talk Out Your Feelings
11. Take a Walk Outside
12. Watch a Movie
13. Read a Book
14. Dance
15. Laugh
16. Paint
17. Sew
18. Draw
19. Go for a Run in Nature
20. Get a Massage
21. Clean and Organize Your Living Space
22. Cook a Fresh Meal
23. Listen to Music
24. Go for a Drive
25. Bike Outside
26. Join a Support Group
27. Hang with a Friend
28. Spend Time with Your Kids
29. Play a Game
30. Build a Fort
31. Do Some Laundry
32. Watch TV
33. Cuddle with a Loved One
34. Write
35. Attend a Social Gathering
36. Join a Workout Class
37. Get a Makeover
38. Take a Yoga Class
39. Go to a Spa

40. Be a Friend
41. Drink Lots of Water
42. Take a Trip
43. Work on Your Routine
44. Eliminate Triggers
45. Learn a New Skill
46. Take a Power Nap
47. Volunteer
48. Smile at a Stranger
49. Hug Someone
50. Donate to a Worthy Cause

Try a handful of these suggestions and add your own.

These may sound like basic suggestions but focusing on the basics will greatly enhance your ability to cope with anxiety. As a result, you will increase your overall quality of life.

Make it easier to manage your bipolar disorder by keeping things simple and utilizing the basics.

Figure out what works for you and add it to your treatment plan.

Adopt the Mentality of a Warrior

PHYSICAL AND MENTAL STRENGTH are characteristics of a warrior. Other characteristics include courage, integrity, inner strength and poise. I strengthen both my mind and body everyday by following my treatment plan.

My treatment plan is a tool, or weapon, for fighting my bipolar disorder. The term fighting can sound exhausting. Especially in a day-in and day-out battle.

Living day-to-day with a mental illness is extremely difficult and tiring. It takes will power, determination and strength to continually deal with a chronic illness like bipolar disorder.

This may sound daunting but it is doable and within your power.

Think of acceptance as your starting point.

Acceptance is one of the most important actions you can take in the long-term management of your bipolar disorder. You must accept that you will be living with bipolar disorder for the rest of your life. Come to terms with this fact as soon as you are able.

You have quite a bit of work cut out for you, but I do not say this to scare you or to create anxiety. In order to know where you want to go, you need to determine where you are presently.

Armed with acceptance and your treatment plan, you have the weapons to fight your bipolar disorder. It will be a daily battle for the rest of your life, but my story is proof that bipolar disorder is manageable with the proper treatment.

If I can do it then know it is in your power to do so, too.

Fighting bipolar disorder is similar to lifting weights. I follow a consistent exercise program to strengthen my muscles. As time goes by, my muscles grow and I can lift heavier weights.

When I first started working out, I found the first few weeks to be extremely hard and exhausting. Once my body adapted to my exercise program, I felt energized and began to push myself harder.

Like working out, it can take time to adapt to your treatment of bipolar disorder. When you are first diagnosed, it is overwhelming and exhausting learning about medication management, self-care practices, and how to manage bipolar disorder for life. Once you find the right treatment plan and successfully manage your bipolar disorder, you will gain energy and focus, as well as have a greater ability to handle stress.

See how similar lifting weights is to the daily treatment of bipolar disorder?

As time goes by, living with bipolar gets easier and easier. It becomes more manageable.

Your mind will grow stronger and your functionality will improve as long as you properly treat your bipolar disorder. You may not be training a muscle like a weightlifter, but you are training your mind to live with bipolar disorder.

Just like a warrior trains his body and mind, you will do the same.

The dictionary defines a *warrior* as, "one who is engaged aggressively or energetically in an activity, cause, or conflict (TheFreeDictionary.com, 2019)."

Living with bipolar disorder defines you as a warrior. A warrior is someone who fights in battle, and you fight the bipolar battle every day of your life.

Yes, you are a warrior, my friend.

It takes courage and skill to live through each day with a mental illness. Your ability to get through each day is a testament to your resolve and ability to survive. If you are reading these words, this means you.

The best way to fight a battle is through preparation and practice.

I choose to see myself as a warrior fighting bipolar disorder; a bipolar warrior.

Empower yourself and do the same.

Managing Your Daily Life with Bipolar Disorder

YOU WILL LIVE WITH BIPOLAR DISORDER for the rest of your life. Plan to take daily steps to improve your ability to manage your illness.

Since bipolar disorder is a complex and serious illness, simplify things and don't make your treatment plan more complicated than it needs to be. This will drastically increase your odds of success in managing your bipolar disorder.

Mastering the basics entails focusing on and implementing healthy activities in your daily life. More than ever, you need to adopt the healthiest lifestyle you can maintain. I simply cannot emphasize this point enough.

The basics include:
- Making healthy eating choices
- Eating at least 3 meals a day
- Exercising daily
- Drinking plenty of water
- Getting enough sleep
- Practicing good personal hygiene
- Not overextending yourself

The best way you can improve your quality of life is to live a healthy one.

Routine

Social Rhythm Therapy is a psychological approach that emphasizes routine. Routine plays an integral part in managing bipolar disorder. The idea is to schedule all your necessary daily activities necessary to function and survive.

For example, schedule the time of day you will take your medication, eat breakfast, lunch and dinner, and your wake time and your bedtime. Add any other activities suitable for your situation.

Create a simple chart with your target time of day along with the corresponding activity you want to accomplish. Add a third column to enter in the actual time you completed the activity. Now, focus on performing each activity at the targeted time. The goal is to schedule your daily activities and follow it as close as possible. This chart will help you to create a daily routine.

Social Rhythm Therapy is based around a similar type of schedule for a baby. If you are a parent with a baby, you know the importance of sticking to an eating and sleeping schedule. An infant must eat at consistent intervals and times throughout the day. Once bedtime or naptime comes around, it is time for your baby to get to sleep.

With Social Rhythm Therapy, you decide the time you want to wake up, go to sleep, eat your meals, and eat your snacks. Your chart will help you to keep track of your routine and follow through with each activity.

You can add whatever activity you want to your chart. Just make sure to create a routine that is doable and realistic.

Medication management and therapy are important components to your routine. Most people do not go to therapy on a daily but generally, weekly basis. It may help you to create two charts: one for your daily routine and the other, for your weekly routine.

Create your daily and weekly chart to help support your treatment of bipolar disorder.

Mastering the basics and routine help those of us living with bipolar disorder.

Prevention Provides Flexibility

Bipolar disorder is not that predictable.

Prevention is a key factor to managing bipolar disorder. The more energy and time you can put into preventing a bipolar mood episode, the greater your chances will be to maintain long-term stability. Following a consistent schedule and routine fosters prevention. Taking control of your own schedule and routine helps put the control of your life back in your hands.

By following your treatment plan and embracing a healthy lifestyle, you are creating a bigger buffer to the stress of daily life.

Random experiences and accidents cannot be predicted. These experiences can increase the stress in your life, and this stress can potentially trigger a manic or depressive episode. Creating a bigger buffer through prevention will help alleviate some of the stress. Increasing your ability to manage stress will help reduce any potential triggers.

There is no way to prepare for everything, but it is in your power to create a healthy mind and body. In turn, this will reduce the fallout of any daily stress and increase your ability to handle this daily stress.

Prevention is a key component to manage bipolar disorder.

Stability, Self-Care, and Coping Strategies

JUST LIKE EACH OF US has a unique biological and chemical makeup, we all have a different baseline for stability.

The doctors and other medical professionals, I have spoken to through the years, agree that an individual living with bipolar can be considered stabilized after one-half to a year of symptom-free living. I have also heard the term "remission" used to indicate stability.

When I say symptom-free, I am talking about the absence of any mood episode. You will continue to experience the general spectrum of emotions and moods like a neurotypical person.

Stability does not mean that your mood will not fluctuate along with your motivation and energy. It just means the intensity of these fluctuations will not greatly impact your daily life. Consistency and routine contribute to the foundation of stability.

The medical model consists of both medication management and therapy. The medical model was the approach I adopted to get initially stabilized. I continue to use this approach as the foundation of my ongoing treatment.

To improve my quality of life, I have discovered coping skills and self-care activities to help get me through the day.

The dictionary defines coping skills as, "...methods a person uses to deal with stressful situations."

Coping strategies fall under the category of healthy and unhealthy. An example of an unhealthy coping strategy is to drink alcohol as the recourse of a sad or stressful event. A positive coping strategy would be to workout when you feel sad or become stressed.

Healthy coping skills enhance your overall quality of life. Unhealthy coping skills will diminish your quality of life.

The following strategies will help to maintain stability and improve your mental health:

1. Medication Management

Medication is the foundation of my treatment plan. I utilize remedies that have been scientifically proven and meticulously studied.

If I do not take my prescribed medication as directed and on a continual basis, I risk getting depressed or manic.

My medication is tweaked by my doctor every so often based on my own symptoms, how I am feeling and my overall functionality.

2. Therapy

Therapy is the second piece to the medical model of treatment. I see my therapist on a weekly basis.

Medication management and therapy are the pillars of my treatment plan.

3. Exercise and Healthy Eating Choices

Exercise and your eating choices are key components in a healthy and stable lifestyle.

Like other aspects of managing your bipolar disorder, make healthy eating choices and exercise daily habits. A healthy lifestyle impacts all other areas of your life, either good or bad.

Leading a healthy lifestyle will enhance your quality of life. You will have a better ability to handle stress, regulate your energy and motivation and improve your mood.

A good place to start is with the basics.

Eat at least three, small, well balanced and well-proportioned meals each day, along with evenly spaced snacks. Try a snack between breakfast and lunch and another between lunch and dinner.

Your meals should consist of a portion of protein, carbohydrate and vegetable. Your snack should consist of a large amount of protein.

I drink at least one protein shake a day. This is generally during one of my snack times. I always drink a protein shake after my workout.

Remember, I am not a registered dietician and not trying to give you actual food advice. I want to give you a framework to start and maintain a healthy lifestyle.

Eating consistently throughout the day is important to maintain proper sugar levels. Maintain a stable sugar level to foster greater stability with your mood, energy level and motivation. You can experience increased mood instability when your sugar levels dip and spike erratically during the course of the day.

Eating systematically throughout the day will also provide you with the necessary energy for your body to function at an efficient level and provide the necessary energy to live an active and healthy lifestyle.

Start making healthy eating choices now!

4. Sleep

Sleep directly impacts your success in managing your bipolar. Healthy sleep hygiene will make your life easier and help you to stabilize. Unhealthy sleep hygiene will destabilize your illness.

Sleep is so important because it can be a trigger. Too little sleep can potentially trigger a manic episode. Too much sleep could signal or potentially trigger, a possible depressive episode.

Make sure you are getting at least 8 hours of sleep. You may have to get more than 8 hours of sleep each night to properly function the following day.

Sleep hygiene consists of how many hours you sleep each night along with a consistent wake time and bedtime. Scheduling both your sleep and wake times will help to structure your routine and sleep schedule. This will help to improve your sleep hygiene.

How did you sleep?

Did you wake up multiple times during the night to use the bathroom or get a drink of water?

When you wake up during the night, can you go right back to sleep or do you lay there trying to sleep?

Some sleep disturbances can be medically diagnosed and treated.

If you still feel groggy, sleepy and like you could sleep for another 6 hours after a full night of sleep, contact your doctor. These symptoms may be indicative of some other medically underlying cause.

See what works best for you.

Following these guidelines will help you feel well-rested and fresh the following morning.

5. Treatment of Other Illnesses

If you are diagnosed with bipolar disorder, may live with a coexisting physical or mental health condition. Examples of these conditions include:

- Heart disease
- Diabetes
- High blood pressure
- High cholesterol
- Sleep disorder (sleep apnea, insomnia or restless leg syndrome)
- Anxiety
- Eating disorder

This list is not exhaustive and barely scratches the surface. Discuss all the possibilities with your doctor and possible testing.

It is extremely overwhelming when you are first diagnosed with bipolar disorder. Having other medical issues only increases stress. We know stress is one of the biggest triggers of a mood episode.

The important thing is to follow the treatment plan.

The mind and body are interconnected. For one to work at its optimal capacity, the other needs to be healthy.

6. Time with Your Loved Ones

Living with bipolar disorder can feel extremely isolating. It is easy to feel alone.

Spending time and connecting with others is important for everyone.

You can join a book club at your local library, meet people online through social media or attend a support group. You can take a class at your local community college or rec center.

Try going to a coffee shop to read a book.

The idea is to be around others. Human interaction is a way to not feel so alone.

7. Aromatherapy and Meditation

I purchased a bamboo diffuser along with a general assortment of oils. I fill the container with distilled water and add 6-8 drops of the oil I am using.

The great thing about a diffuser is you can mix oils together in the diffuser or use one type of oil by itself. There are also premade mixtures that you can purchase.

Experiment with the various oils and see which ones energize you or calm you down.

You can practice mediation in tandem with aromatherapy or by itself.

Meditation is a great way to center your mind and body. It does not have to be a big drawn out event.

Purchase a CD with different meditation techniques.

Pull up YouTube or Google and search on your phone or computer. Simply enter "meditation [timeframe]". For example, for a 10-minute meditation, enter "meditation 10-minutes".

Set your intention for the day with a morning session. The evening is an important time to help you wind down from the day. Add shorter meditation sessions throughout the day during breaks, at work, and lunch. See what fits your schedule and stick to it.

Think about adding more smaller sessions throughout the day if your stress level increases.

8. Drinking Water

An adult body is made up of anywhere from 55%-65% of water. It is dependent on your age, gender, activity level, environment, and stress.

To help keep your body and organs functioning at their optimal level, you need to drink water on a daily and consistent basis.

The recommendation on the amount of water to drink changes, but I try to shoot for 8 glasses of water consisting of 8 ounces each glass.

I try to drink more water because the medications I take have side effects. Some medications can actually become toxic if you do not drink enough water. Drinking water helps to flush the toxins out of my system and keep my body running at an efficient level. The last thing I need is to further tax my body.

Find out all the information you can about each medication you take.

Make sure to drink plenty of water each day.

Last Thoughts

Stability can seem like an elusive concept when you are first diagnosed. Like anything worth doing in life, it takes hard work and commitment.

Don't be disillusioned with the idea that you can do "x" or "y" and you will be better. To find a quality of life that you can live with and manage, you need to experiment with different self-care activities.

You will probably find it necessary to adopt a number of different strategies to manage your illness.

Just remember, stability is not some far-fetched idea.

Stability is within your reach.

Classes of Medication

Mood Stabilizers

The primary focus of mood stabilizers is mood stabilization. Extreme mood instability is a hallmark of bipolar disorder. Mood stabilizers help to even out the roller coaster in a person's mood cycling.

Sometimes patients will be prescribed multiple mood stabilizers. Some stabilizers work on different pathways in the brain. For example, anticonvulsants are a subclass of mood stabilizers. Anticonvulsants reduce the incidence of seizures but have been shown to have mood stabilizing effects.

Lithium was one of the first mood stabilizers and is a natural salt. Like many other medications to treat bipolar disorder, lithium requires blood tests for continual monitoring.

Antipsychotics

Antipsychotics are used to treat psychosis, namely, hallucinations and delusions. They are also prescribed for disordered thinking. They work quickly and have a more sedating effect compared to mood stabilizers. This helps to bring a patient down from the high and intensity of a manic episode.

There are two subclasses of antipsychotics called typical and atypical antipsychotics.

Typical antipsychotics are the older and first generation antipsychotics. They generally have a higher incidence of side effects and are not as easily tolerated. For this line of reasoning, they are not currently a primary weapon to fight bipolar disorder.

Atypical antipsychotics are the new generation of antipsychotics. They are supposed to have a smaller amount of side effects and to be better tolerated than their typical predecessors. Atypical antipsychotics are currently the primary level of attack when it comes to psychotic symptoms.

Sleep Aids

Sleep aids are generally not prescribed for longer than 7 days. They are highly addictive, and your body can build up a tolerance to them over time.

On a rare occasion a doctor may prescribe a patient a sleep aid to take for longer than 7 days. Each individual is a unique case.

Sleep aids are not a first line of attack for those diagnosed with bipolar disorder. Sleep aids are looked at as a possibility when other avenues of treatment are exhausted.

Antidepressants

Antidepressants are a class of medication used as a primary treatment in unipolar depression.

As a last resort, a doctor may prescribe an antidepressant for bipolar depression. An individual with bipolar type 1 can be thrown into a manic episode if given an antidepressant. I know this from firsthand experience.

In addition to decreasing depression, many antidepressants help to reduce the symptoms of anxiety.

Some antidepressants have a synergistic effect with another medication such as an antipsychotic or other class of medication. A synergistic effect means that both medications work together to improve their overall functionality and reduce their side effect profile.

Stimulants

Stimulants are a class of medication that are almost never prescribed for bipolar disorder. This is especially true for bipolar disorder type 1. Stimulants can put your brain into overdrive and trigger a manic episode.

Stimulants are primarily prescribed for ADD and ADHD. In some cases, a patient can be diagnosed with both bipolar disorder and ADD or ADHD. Managing these two conditions together in one case is difficult but can be done.

Presently, there are newer alternatives to the older generation of stimulants. These newer medications primarily treat inattentiveness and inability to concentrate while reducing the stimulating effects of the older generation of stimulants. This is a fantastic alternative for those of us living with bipolar disorder.

Last Thoughts

Prescribing medication is a process of trial and error. There is no test to determine the proper medication or medication cocktail. It really is a crapshoot and can take years to find the proper combination. It is quite normal to feel like a guinea pig.

I do not want to discourage you, but it took me close to a decade to find a tolerable medication regimen. In my case, I am extremely sensitive to medication and their many side effects. Plus, a positive quality of life is extremely important to me. These two variables combined made it difficult for me to find a tolerable combination of medications.

Since I take a number of pills at various times during the day, I use a weekly pill container. I can divide my medication over 7 days and at various times throughout the day.

You should always lock up your medication. I have a safe to lock up my meds and this protects my kids. The safe also protects myself in times of crisis.

A medication container is a great way to support medication adherence. It is a fantastic tool to keep your meds organized and all in one place.

My friend uses a special medication container. It administers their medication with the use of a timer. The timer goes off at preset times throughout the day. It actually releases the medication after the timer buzzes. This is a great option if you are having problems with remembering your medication.

Always (and I mean ALWAYS) stay on your medication. One time I went off my meds, and I immediately went into a manic episode.

Never stop your medication cold turkey. You can experience horrible side effects and withdrawals with various medications when you abruptly stop them. This also increases the likelihood of triggering an episode.

If you are tapering down on a medication or stopping one completely, make sure your doctor closely supervises this change.

Nowadays, there is a movement to be med free. It can be life threatening to join this bandwagon. I need medication to function.

Pill shaming is another movement that coincides with the med free movement. Pill shaming takes place when someone chastises others because they take medication.

Like diabetes or cancer, bipolar disorder is a chronic illness requiring medication to properly treat it.

Please remember to speak with your doctor before making any medication changes.

Weight Gain with Psychotropic Medication

WEIGHT GAIN IS ONE OF THE biggest potential side effects from bipolar medications.

Everyone is biologically unique. Because of this, no two individuals will react the same way to medication. You can give the same medication to two different individuals and one may gain weight and the other may lose weight.

Improving my quality of life is one of my long-term goals in the treatment of my bipolar disorder. Gaining weight is contradictory to this goal because it decreases my quality of life.

I will take a medication that causes weight gain on a short-term basis and in an acute situation. If the medication is needed for a long-term period, I make sure to watch my food choices and get as much exercise as I can handle.

I have my own baseline of side effects when it comes to my medication. You need to determine what is acceptable in your own treatment. Do not let a medical professional or other individual dictate your boundaries if you are not comfortable with the approach. After all, it is your life and your body.

Let me give you an example regarding my baseline of side effects.

There is a subclass of medication that causes me to gain weight each time I use it. When I say weight gain, it is not a couple of pounds here or there. One time, I gained close to 50 pounds in a timeframe of only a couple of months. This is not okay with me.

Others have commented, "wouldn't you rather be overweight than dead?" Personally, I find this line of thinking counterproductive. Gaining unnecessary weight creates a host of other side effects and issues.

You have to decide what is acceptable in your own treatment plan.

There are so many options of medications. You do not have to settle for a particular med if you can't stand the side effects. Discuss your options with your doctor and come up with a game plan.

This is your life. If you don't like the treatment approach, voice your concern. You are paying a medical professional to help you. They are the expert to treat you, but you are the expert of your own life.

The relationship you have with your doctor is a collaboration. Your doctor's philosophy of treatment should be in line with your own.

One time, a doctor's treatment philosophy did not coincide with my own personal beliefs.

I remember I saw him for close to two years. When the opportunity opened up for me to change to a new doctor, I jumped at the chance without looking back.

Make sure you understand the direction your doctor is taking in your treatment plan. Keep an open line of communication with them and always feel free to speak up.

If you do have issues gaining weight on a medication, speak with your doctor to rule out other possible medical problems. If your thyroid isn't working properly, weight gain could be a direct result. You gain weight even if you watch what you eat and exercise regularly.

Once I discontinued the medication that made me gain 50 pounds, I stopped putting on weight. To work off the extra pounds, I made healthy eating choices and followed my workout program.

You are the only one who can determine your own baseline for side effects. As part of your treatment plan, discuss your baseline with your doctor and loved ones.

Therapy is a Component to Recovery

THERAPY IS THE OTHER COMPONENT to the medical model. It works in tandem with medication management.

Find a therapist with whom you connect. Make sure you feel comfortable and open with the person you choose to be your therapist. If you aren't happy with your choice, find another one.

The relationship I have with my therapist is more important than the actual type of therapy.

Let's take a look at the different therapy modalities.

Types of Therapy

CBT

Cognitive Behavioral Therapy is a practical approach to psychotherapy. It's focus is to positively change patterns of behavior and thinking. You may have heard it referred to as "talk therapy."

It is a popular form of therapy for an individual going through a rough patch in their life. For example, situational depression is quite common. There is usually a short-term goal that once reached can end the need for further psychotherapy.

Bipolar disorder is a chronic illness that you can't simply work through and get better. I support the medical model of treatment and plan to participate in cognitive behavioral therapy for the rest of my life.

DBT

Dialectical Behavioral Therapy is an evidence-based approach to psychotherapy. It was originally developed to help those living with borderline personality disorder, but it can be used to treat mood disorders such as bipolar disorder.

Group Skills classes and individual psychotherapy are components of dialectical behavioral therapy.

DBT focuses on 4 major areas:

1. *Distress Tolerance* is a coping skill used to help a person get through a crisis.
2. *Mindfulness* is the focus of one's attention on the present moment.
3. *Interpersonal Effectiveness* encompasses the skills to create and maintain positive relationships with others.
4. *Emotion Regulation* is a way to manage and regulate your own emotions in response to a particular situation.

EMDR

Eye Movement Desensitization and Reprocessing is a non-traditional form of psychotherapy. It was originally developed for patients living with post-traumatic stress disorder (PTSD).

During the process, individuals learn how to move past their trauma.

Skills are developed to better cope with any potentially triggering situations and deal with any lingering trauma.

There are a number of other different therapies.

CBT, DBT and EMDR are psychological approaches commonly used today.

I have extensive experience with CBT and DBT. They have both helped me tremendously along my journey. My personal experience with EMDR is extremely limited.

When studying the medical model, most studies used medication management and cognitive behavioral therapy.

In the end, find someone you connect with and feel comfortable sharing your feelings.

Your Support System

A SUPPORT SYSTEM is an integral part of treatment.

Most people think of friends and family when they think of a support system. You can enlist the support of anybody in your network of contacts. There is no built-in rule.

One of the reasons I believe in the medical model so much is the built-in support you receive from the medical community. You gain two medical professionals to add to your support system. Both your doctor and therapist will be there for you in times of crisis and stability.

A psychiatrist, psychiatric nurse practitioner, or other licensed medical professional prescribes your medication. A therapist walks you through whichever mode of therapy you have chosen. These two medical professionals will be with you through the long haul.

If you have a group of supportive friends and family, that is great. Unfortunately, not everyone has that luxury.

In the past couple of years, I have learned the importance of having people in your life that do not destabilize your bipolar disorder.

Would you rather:
a) have a support system full of people that contribute drama and provide a potential trigger or,
b) have less people around, but with no triggers?

Whichever scenario you choose will ultimately determine how hard of a road you will travel.

I used to be the guy in scenario a).

I learned the importance of reducing the drama, toxic relationships, and triggers in my life. Now, I have much more control over my triggers. I no longer deal with toxic relationships.

In addition to my medical support team, a handful of close friends and family comprise my support system.

Carefully choose the individuals you allow in your circle of support. Do you value and respect their advice? Is it a give-and-take relationship or take, take, take? Make sure the individuals you allow in your circle build you up and not tear you down.

Have you heard of blind loyalty?

Blind loyalty is supporting and backing a person no matter what they have done.

You don't owe anybody, including family, anything. Just because you played a specific role in a person's life, doesn't mean you are required to continue doing so. If a particular person is triggering to you, cut them out of your circle. Your future self will thank you for it later.

Lean more on your therapist and psychiatrist or nurse practitioner if you don't have many close friends or family. There is nothing wrong with that. In fact, isn't that one of the reasons they are a part of your support team?

Reach out if you feel compelled to do so. Join a group at church if you are religious. If a certain sport is your thing, join a sports team. You can also take a class at your YMCA or other local organization.

There are numerous websites where you can make friends, find workout partners or find a romantic connection. With the arrival of the digital age, you can meet people from all over the world without leaving your home. Always protect yourself first and foremost. Be careful if you choose to divulge personal information online. Never put yourself in a compromising or unsafe situation.

Find a Support Group

SUPPORT GROUPS ARE a fantastic way to meet others living with bipolar disorder.

Support groups are not group therapy. They are generally peer led. Group therapy is run by a therapist or other medical professional.

There are a number of different organizations that facilitate support groups.

Have you heard of NAMI, the National Alliance on Mental Illness?

What about DBSA, the Depression and Bipolar Support Alliance?

NAMI and DBSA are wonderful organizations that provide support nationwide. You can generally find a support group, from one of these two organizations, close to the area that you reside.

With the electronic age, you have a couple options as to how you would like to attend a support group.

The traditional in-person support group is available but so is an online support group.

In-person Support Group

An in-person support group is great if you enjoy physically being around others and meeting new people in-person.

A schedule is created by the facilitators or the individuals running the support group. A group can meet once a week, every other week, once a month or some other predetermined time frame. In addition, groups can run 30 minutes long up to a couple hours.

The time and location are determined by the organizers.

The downsides to an in-person support group include the meeting time and physical location. There is no flexibility with the scheduled meeting time, unless the facilitators have pre-planned for a change. If you miss one week, you just go to the next scheduled meeting. You can't simply reschedule a group meeting at the last minute for another time during the week.

When I ran my support group, we met every other week with each session lasting about an hour and a half.

Online Support Group

The inflexibility of time and location of an in-person support group is remedied by the functionality of an online support group. Most online support groups consist of a chat room and discussion board. You can go and come as you please with a chat room or forum. With a discussion board, you post your thoughts when you feel like it.

This is a great option if you are busy or do not leave your home on a regular basis.

You don't get to meet others face-to-face, but some online support groups are enlisting video options for their groups. With the availability of video streaming, you can see the person or people to whom you are speaking.

An online support group can also provide a certain level of anonymity.

Ask yourself a couple of questions to help decide which group would better fit your personality and situation.

Do you enjoy the physical company of others?

Would a degree of anonymity be good?

Is a concrete schedule best for your situation or would you rather have some flexibility?

Ask these questions and investigate. This will help you decide if an in-person or online support group would best suit you. I suggest trying both.

Being a member of a support group is a great adjunct to your treatment plan. It's a great way to share your story, hear the stories of others and support one another traversing the same road.

Make Exercise a Priority

EXERCISE HAS BEEN INSTRUMENTAL in managing my bipolar disorder. In fact, I feel following an exercise plan is absolutely imperative to the long-term management of bipolar disorder. For me, it is a daily non-negotiable.

In my treatment plan, daily exercise comes next in importance after taking my medication and seeing a therapist on a regular basis.

Working out has both natural mood stabilizing and antidepressant effects. Just remember, exercise doesn't take the place of your medication.

Making healthy eating choices and exercising regularly both foster a healthy lifestyle. A healthy lifestyle will result in the highest level operating mind and body.

Each decision you make in the course of the day will have a direct impact on your bipolar disorder. Make good choices and you'll help manage your bipolar disorder.

Throughout my life, I have enjoyed an active lifestyle. There have been many peaks and valleys along my journey. Most of my roller coaster ride regarding exercise adherence is on account of my bipolar disorder.

Those of us living with bipolar disorder are at a greater risk for heart disease, high blood pressure and cholesterol, diabetes and other physical conditions. Exercise is one of the top preventative measures you can take to battle these maladies.

If you live with physical conditions, talk to your doctor and physical therapist about your limitations. They can help you determine your options regarding exercise programs. It goes without saying, but please speak with your doctor before starting any workout program.

If you are a beginner, start with 20 minutes of light exercise each day. Even as little as 20 minutes of exercise has been shown to have positive benefits. The important thing is to get moving.

Anything that elevates your heart rate for that minimum threshold of 20 minutes counts. A simple light walk is enough. Maybe you enjoy swimming or biking. I love weight lifting. Weight lifting is my daily exercise. I also enjoy biking, running and swimming.

If you are having a hard time finding an activity, stop by your local library and check out their selection of workout DVDs. There are many at-home workout programs and yoga DVDs available. It's a great alternative if you can't afford the monthly price of a membership to a gym.

When depressed, your doctor and therapist generally recommend exercise. This may seem counterintuitive.

How can you take action when movement is the last thing you want to do while depressed? The answer is to start exercising and make it a daily habit before you become depressed.

Start a workout program when you are in a stable state of mind. Once exercise becomes a daily habit, you will increase your odds of sticking to it. That way if you do slide into a depressive state, exercise will already be one of your daily habits. You will only have to focus on going through the motions of your workout.

To make exercise a habit, commit to a realistic workout program and stick to it.

Routine has always been difficult for me on account of bipolar disorder. My motivation, activity level and mood, rise and ebb with the flow of my illness. I know from my experience I cannot start exercising during a depressive episode, if it is not already a habit.

You can train your body to expect a certain amount of activity. That way, even if you are not motivated or don't have the energy, you can still go through the motions. Something is always better than nothing.

Aerobic exercise has many mood stabilizing effects because it floods your body with endorphins and other positive mood-enhancing hormones. Your body responds in a similar fashion to anaerobic exercise.

Have you ever had a "runner's high"? It is the way the body can react after a strenuous run. Endorphins are surging through your body giving you that "high" feeling. You can experience a similar feeling after an intense weight lifting session.

I love lifting weights. It is an example of anaerobic exercise. I learned how to lift back in high school, and I enjoy it to this day!

When I am in a good state of mind, I can push myself, focus on each rep and record my progress. The opposite occurs when my mood starts to dip. My motivation wanes and I feel like doing nothing. I may not have the drive and focus that I have when I am feeling ok, but I can still get a workout in. I make it a priority to at least workout at home.

If you have an issue with workout adherence, enlist a workout partner or try an exercise class. Join a team sport such as soccer, softball, or tennis.

There are so many benefits to working out. For the management of bipolar disorder, exercise helps mood regulation, improve sleep, increase self-confidence, and improve your quality of life.

Potential benefits of exercise include:
- Longer periods of focus
- Increase in neurochemicals that foster brain health repair
- Memory improvement
- Increase in energy level
- Healthy quality of sleep
- Reduction in anxiety
- Lower blood pressure
- Weight loss

- Faster metabolism
- Boost in sex drive
- Increased strength
- Stronger bones
- The growth of blood vessels and new nerve cells
- Decrease in your risk of chronic disease
- Reduction in pain

My journey with bipolar disorder has provided many opportunities to learn. This includes lessons about living a healthy lifestyle.

Consistency is Paramount to a Healthy Lifestyle

Daily healthy action needs to take place to live a healthy lifestyle. Do not adopt the mentality of the *weekend warrior*. You need to make good eating choices and exercise every day.

Prioritize your workout each day. I tell myself I will not go to sleep at night until I finish my minimum 20 minutes of daily exercise.

Engage in some kind of daily activity. If you can't get in your total workout, something is always better than nothing.

Look at daily exercise as small deposits to your mental health and physical health bank. A little bit each day adds up to a lot over the long haul.

Balance Should be Your Focus

Focus on balance and moderation when making healthy eating choices.

We know that bipolar disorder is an illness of extremes. Balance is a tool you need in your arsenal of coping techniques. Balance will help to lessen the extreme nature of bipolar disorder.

Eat in moderation by watching the portion sizes of your meals. Do your best not to overindulge.

Eat smaller meals throughout the day at consistent intervals. This will help to maintain your sugar level. A sugar level too high or too low can increase anxiety, mood instability, irritability, and daytime sleepiness.

Again, focus on balance.

Stop the Black and White Thinking

In the past, I viewed my eating choices and workouts as all-or-nothing. If I missed one day of working out or ate an unhealthy snack, I felt it completely derailed my progress.

Living a healthy lifestyle is no easy task. I guarantee there will be bumps in the road. After I realized this, I was able to get rid of the all-or-nothing thinking.

Try looking at your journey in hues of gray. If you miss a workout or don't have a great day of eating, don't punish yourself. Just get back on the wagon the next day. You'll increase your mental strength by getting back on track after getting knocked down.

Remember, something is always better than nothing. If you can only get in 10 minutes of a workout, do it. Try your hardest not to skip a day. Just remember it does happen.

Don't find and make excuses.

Take action and do it.

No Crash Diets

Maintaining a diet over the long haul is not realistic. You may be able to follow a certain diet over a couple of weeks or even a number of months. Most of the time these so-called diets will restrict something in your eating habits like a certain kind or type of food. Restricting or eliminating certain kinds of foods isn't conducive to your long-term success.

Restricting or overindulging will only tilt the scales. In the long-run, a crash diet will only make your journey more difficult.

Always remember one of our favorite terms: moderation.

Live a healthy lifestyle by making good food choices and exercising regularly.

Your mind and body will thank you.

Electroconvulsive Therapy (ECT) On the Brain

I WAS FIRST INTRODUCED to electroconvulsive therapy in the early 2000s.

During one of my hospital stays, a doctor specializing in ECT consulted with me. He felt ECT would have a positive impact on the treatment of my bipolar disorder and was my best option.

When I first spoke to the ECT doctor, he did a great job of answering my questions and putting my family and myself at ease. He mentioned the possible side effects of temporary memory loss, aches, pains, and headaches. He explained my long-term memory would not be affected.

He explained the procedure along with all the safety precautions, possible outcomes and again, potential side effects.

I was in an extremely bad spot at this time in my life. Suicidal ideation filled my thoughts on a continual basis. I couldn't get out of bed or function. I progressively got worse and worse.

In the end, keeping myself alive outweighed any potential negative side effects.

ECT isn't a primary line of attack in an individual's treatment. I tried a number of different medications and treatments before I ultimately decided to try ECT.

Over the course of about 5 years, I had a total of around 55 ECT sessions.

People liken depression to sadness. Everyone experiences sadness throughout their lives. Depression is an illness that can only be diagnosed by a doctor or equivalent medical professional.

Depression swallows your soul. It sucks the energy out of your life to the point where you cannot function.

In the early to mid-2000s I could not function, and I decided to try ECT treatments.

Electroconvulsive therapy is not like it used to be. I'm sure you've seen it portrayed in pop culture movies as a primitive and barbaric act. Now, there are fewer side effects and a muscle relaxant is used to stop almost all movement during the procedure.

The schedule is generally Monday, Wednesday, and Friday early in the morning for a few weeks at a time. If I remember correctly, maintenance ECTs are once a month.

Upon arriving in the pre-op area, I filled out a memory form with basic questions covering cognitive abilities. An ECT nurse took my vitals.

After putting on a hospital gown, the nurse pushed me into the procedure room on a hospital bed. The nurse positioned me on the bed for the ECT treatment, and my doctor put in an IV catheter.

My doctor administered a muscle relaxant with a host of other medications, and I quickly fell asleep.

I was given a bilateral ECT treatment. After I was anesthetized, my doctor put an electrode on each of my temples. Electricity passed through my brain, between each electrode, and initiated a seizure. The doctor monitored my seizure on his machine. The only way you could visually tell I was having a seizure was my little toe twitched.

I awoke to a nurse telling me I was in recovery and already had my ECT treatment. My memory is extremely fuzzy about this step in the process, but I remember having oxygen and taking a memory and cognitive function test.

My doctors explained to me that I would regain my short-term memory. They assured me there wouldn't be any long-term effects on my memory. Unfortunately, the treatments did mess up my memory.

To this day, I cannot recall events during this period of time. I have pieced together what occurred based on the reflections of my family and friends. I also have a few fuzzy memories that make sense after chatting with my loved ones.

I had dozens of notebooks full of class notes, homework and labs. It is quite scary that they were all in my own handwriting, and I can't recollect even one word, drawing, or diagram. The ECT treatments basically erased my chemical engineering education from my memory.

I kept all of my papers, notebooks, problems, and labs for years. Every so often I would go back to see if I could remember anything. That was never the case.

Losing the memory of my engineering schooling (along with other memories during that time period) was devastating. Especially when I had friends, family members, and teachers question my reasoning for halting my efforts to complete my chemical engineering. It was a different time back then, and I kept the part of my life regarding bipolar disorder a secret.

The good news is that I completed so many math and chemistry classes that I was close to a Natural Sciences degree. I only had to finish a couple math classes. I earned my B.S. in Natural Sciences with minors in both Math and Chemistry, in 2004.

I don't feel regret because in the end, I earned a bachelor's degree, lived to tell the tale, and had a better idea how to manage my bipolar disorder. I am also a father to two wonderful kids and husband to the love of my life. Pretty cool, considering I thought I would not make it to my 30th birthday.

I am a firm believer in doing your best, with what you have, at that particular time. That is one of the reasons I do not feel bitter or harbor anger regarding my experience with ECT.

It is always easier to blame an issue on someone or something else. That kind of thinking has always brought me down.

For me, ECT was a last-ditch effort to save my life, and it did. For me, that is enough to celebrate. I can honestly say that I wouldn't be here today if it had not been for my ECT treatments.

If you are trying to decide if ECT treatments are right for you, look at the pros and cons. Just like medications, ECT has potential side effects.

Does the possibility of getting better outweigh the risks?

I can't answer that for you.

ECT treatments saved my life. When it comes to the question of should I or should I not go through ECT treatments, I'm grateful I opted to go through them.

I'll never get my memories back. For me, that is ok. I am beyond grateful for the life I have.

What Are Your Expectations?

WE ALL PERCEIVE our own actions and those of others through our own eyes. This perception is crafted through the lens of our own experience and expectations.

We all have people in our lives. Each person plays a specific role.

For me, I am a father, husband, blogger, author, friend, brother, cousin, acquaintance, and stranger. For each of these roles, I have my own set of expectations about how I function. Those around me have their own expectations about how I fill that role in their life. When these expectations coincide for myself and others, both sides win.

I have always had high expectations of myself. That will never change.

Looking at my past, I can now see that I did not expect much from those around me.

For the vast majority of my life I felt that people did not live up to my high expectations. I have since come to realize that it wasn't my high expectations of others that left me disappointed, but that I actually had little to no expectations of others.

Having no expectations of another person allows them the ability to treat you however they want. If you have no expectations, you do not have a set of standards by which to compare.

I have since learned that if people do not meet my expectations I can either:
a) Cut them out of my life
b) Expect that they will treat me below my acceptable standards

I have chosen to raise my expectations of others. I choose who I allow into my inner circle.

This new eye-opening realization pinpointed various triggering and toxic relationships. To create and maintain stability of my bipolar disorder, I had to cut these relationships out of my life.

Again, others have their own expectations of how I should act and play a specific role in their own lives. I no longer feel bad about raising my expectations of others. Managing my bipolar disorder is more important than the way I "should" be acting.

My health and ability to function is more important than anything else. If that upsets someone, so be it.

Now I focus on those relationships that are fulfilling, healthy and important to me. These relationships build me up and don't tear me down.

Should I expect more from you?

No, I will never expect more from you than I do of myself.

Don't lower your expectations or eliminate them altogether at the expense of your own health and stability.

Stigma is Real

THERE ARE COUNTLESS EXAMPLES OF STIGMA.

When a violent crime is committed by a person, the general public automatically assumes the person is mentally ill. The opposite is that every person living with a mental illness, like bipolar disorder, is violent. This is in fact untrue. The vast majority of individuals with bipolar disorder are not violent. Those living with bipolar disorder who commit crimes generally are not properly medicated.

Ignorance and fear both fan the flames of stigma.

Broadening the definition of bipolar disorder increases the number of diagnosed cases because the definition encompasses more people. This leaves more room for human error.

Stigma has a negative connotation and permeates through all of society. The dictionary defines stigma as "a mark of disgrace associated with a particular circumstance, quality, or person (Lexico Dictionaries | English, 2019)."

The way you say something can contribute to the stigma regarding bipolar disorder. It is important to think before you speak. Some people do not realize the ramifications of their own words. Words can do more harm than good if used in the wrong way. How you use your words, positively or negatively, impacts those around you.

The seriousness of bipolar disorder has been minimized through its use in pop culture. Weather forecasters commonly state, "the weather is bipolar". When someone is moody, "they are acting bipolar." This further minimizes the intensity and serious nature of bipolar disorder.

Recently, more and more celebrities are disclosing their diagnosis of bipolar disorder. Pop culture seems to sensationalize living with bipolar disorder. It seems almost like the "cool" or "in" thing to have bipolar disorder.

I'm not sure why someone would want to have bipolar disorder. I guess when something is trendy with celebrities, people just want to follow along.

It is silly to me.

Never give ignorance a hall pass. Stand up and correct those who do not understand. We can combat stigma by educating those who don't understand bipolar disorder.

Living with bipolar disorder, we have a big responsibility.

It is important that we lead by example. I do this by successfully managing my bipolar disorder on a daily basis. I take my medication as directed, exercise daily, maintain healthy habits, and implement positive coping strategies.

Taking personal responsibility for my bipolar disorder is one of the ways I combat stigma. Never underestimate your impact as an individual.

Don't believe anybody who says that there's a cure for bipolar disorder. Unfortunately, right now, there is no cure. However, you can successfully manage it with the proper treatment.

Think of bipolar disorder as a spectrum. The strongest symptomatology of bipolar disorder is at one end. As you go to the other end, the strength of your symptoms decreases. An individual living with bipolar disorder will experience a spectrum of symptoms during the life of their illness.

A bipolar diagnosis indicates that you experience difficulty functioning. Bipolar disorder is a serious illness that directly impacts your daily living, mood, energy, and motivation. If you can manage your life without proper treatment, then you are experiencing the normal ups and downs of daily life.

My suggestion is to get another opinion if this happens to you. Make sure that you receive the correct diagnosis. Over the course of my life, I have seen more than 15 doctors who have independently diagnosed me with bipolar disorder type 1.

Pill shaming is a harmful movement in our current society. Those of us trying to fight our illness with medication are looked at as weak and padding the pockets of big pharma.

Anyone you speak with is likely to have had a bad experience with medication. It's completely understandable because it took me years to find a combination of meds that worked. I just kept working with my doctor until I found an acceptable med cocktail.

The mental health system is overextended with little resources compared to the gross amount of patients. Doctors don't have enough time to spend with their patients.

I understand some people have bad experiences with medication. The side effects can be extremely debilitating. I've been there and know what it feels like to be a guinea pig.

Shaming those of us trying to manage our bipolar disorder further contributes to stigma. Those that require medication may not come forward for treatment because of this stigma.

Conspiracy theories also perpetuate stigma. I recently heard a theory that Big Pharma is getting us addicted to our psychotropic medications, so we have to pay more money.

We can talk about conspiracies, bad experiences and all sorts of negative stuff. The fact is that medication has proven to help manage bipolar disorder. Especially the most severe cases.

If I don't take my medication, I will get manic, depressed or experience a mixed state. My medications are part of the foundation of my stability and treatment.

It's your choice if you don't support the use of medication. Just don't put me down. I spent close to a decade finding a workable cocktail of meds.

Was it exhausting?

Yes.

Did it take persistence?

Yes.

Did I want to give up?

Yes, many times I felt like it.
Was it worth the work and effort?
Yes, I can actually function and live my life!

Common Frustrating Statements

People calling me "Crazy"

Crazy is a term that contributes to the stigma surrounding mental illness.

To me, it feels like we are teleported back in time to the poorly kept institutions and asylums for the mentally ill.

"Crazy" has a negative connotation in pop culture. People use the word "crazy" to describe erratic behavior, a far-fetched idea, and criminal behavior. That is why "crazy" has a negative connotation. It is hurtful to use this terminology to describe someone living with a mental illness.

Next time think before you speak.

Words don't break bones but they can hurt your mental health.

"We all have a little bipolar in each of us."

I have heard this statement more times than I can count. It is an uneducated remark and minimizes the journey of those of us living with bipolar disorder.

I understand the premise behind the statement. Since everyone has ups and downs, they must have some bipolar disorder, right? Wrong!

Bipolar disorder is a mental illness based on extremes. These extremes cycle between mania and depression, energy, motivation, and changes in activity level. These symptoms can negatively impact your daily life to the point where you can't function. Relationships, finances, and work are all directly affected. These are not the normal ups and downs a person without bipolar disorder experiences on a daily basis.

In serious situations, you can even be incarcerated due to the extreme nature of bipolar disorder.

In a worst-case scenario, you can die.

No, everyone does not have a little bipolar in them.

"It is all in your head."

The implication is that the person living with bipolar disorder can change their thoughts and be better. Further, bipolar disorder is not real, and only exists in the afflicted individual's mind. Hence, "It is all in your head."

When someone cuts their head open and you can see blood, it is obvious that something is wrong. Bipolar disorder is an invisible illness because you cannot see it with the naked eye, but it is there.

Presently, there is no test that can diagnose bipolar disorder. A doctor has to use their knowledge and clinical assessment to properly diagnose bipolar disorder.

Just because you can't see it, does not mean it isn't there.

"You have control over this."

This statement is similar in perspective to, "It is all in your head". A neurotypical individual does not have a mental illness such as bipolar disorder. If you live with a chemically balanced brain, you can use affirmations to make yourself feel better and to change your thought process. Again, this is true for a neurotypical person.

Unfortunately, this is not the case for those of us living with bipolar disorder. You can never "will" yourself into a better mood with bipolar disorder. There is no way to simply snap out of a manic episode or think good thoughts and no longer be depressed.

Thinking along those lines can be very dangerous to someone diagnosed with bipolar disorder.

In life, we only have a certain amount of control. For instance, you can control how you react to a situation. This is only true if you are a neurotypical individual or your bipolar is stabilized.

With bipolar disorder, it can feel like you don't have control. Bipolar disorder can take control of both your thoughts and emotions. While manic or depressed you cannot control how you react to a situation. Bipolar does that for you.

The best thing you can do is to take healthy action in managing your illness. You can do this by finding a suitable treatment plan and taking preventative measures to reduce both manic and depressive episodes.

What Is a Trigger?

THE DICTIONARY DEFINES A TRIGGER as, "an event or circumstance that is the cause of a particular action, process, or situation (especially of something read, seen, or heard) distress (someone), typically as a result of arousing feelings or memories associated with a particular traumatic experience (Lexico Dictionaries | English, 2019)."

A trigger can spark either a manic or depressive episode.

Triggers can be anything.

A friend or a family member can be a trigger. These types of relationships are generally extremely toxic. Is it worth sabotaging your mental health to maintain this relationship?

Either cut ties or reduce the impact of these relationships.

To manage your bipolar disorder long-term, you need to put your health first. If your mind is sick, how can you function in your daily life?

Your mental health must go above and beyond your desire to maintain any kind of relationship. When you accept this, then and only then will you be able to cut the toxic people out of your life. It will not matter if they are a friend, family member or other loved one.

Never let someone guilt you into staying with them or continuing the relationship if you know they are a trigger. Trust me, there are more than enough people in this world to take their place.

This may seem cruel, but I have learned firsthand the benefits of cutting toxic relationships out of my life. Putting yourself first is part of self-love. It is not selfish to put your health and well-being first.

My last manic episode was back in November of 2016. Toxic relationships in my life partly triggered this episode. It's a good thing I cut these toxic relationships out of my life. This is the longest time I have gone without a manic episode.

It comes down to the question:
Do you want to be healthy or not?

You may have the desire, but you must take action. Even if this action makes you uncomfortable, realize the importance to your long-term stability.

Relationships are tricky. Certain expectations may be set with which you do not necessarily agree but have maintained for a length of time.

It is not a requirement in "life's handbook" for you to have a relationship with anyone you feel is a trigger of your bipolar disorder. The point is if you feel they are toxic or a trigger, cut them out of your life.

You don't owe anyone anything, and I can bet they feel the same too.

Sometimes a trigger can be an image. If you have this trigger, you need to be very careful what you watch on TV, at the movies, and what's around you. Pay attention to your social media accounts and what you look at on the internet.

Triggers can also be a situation, a smell, a feeling, or touch. If you can cut these triggers out of your life, do it. If you can't cut them out, do your best to reduce their impact on your life.

Either way, focus on prevention to create a buffer against these triggers.

Types of Triggers Defined

THERE ARE SOME COMMON TRIGGERS when you live with bipolar disorder.

Just because you experience one of the following triggers doesn't mean it will initiate an actual mood episode. Be aware of your own bipolar disorder and what can potentially trigger a manic or depressive episode for you.

You will be at a greater advantage to manage your bipolar disorder if you are self-aware of what can worsen your illness.

1. Stress

Everybody experiences stress. There is no way to get rid of it, but you can manage stress just like you can manage your bipolar disorder.

If you look at any trigger, you will see they stem from stress on the mind and/or body. Focus on managing the stress in your life and reducing it.

My therapist described to me a very useful metaphor about stress that I would like to share with you.

Look at your ability to cope with stress as a cup. We all have different sized cups because we all have different abilities to cope with stress.

The liquid that fills this cup are triggers and stressful situations. The amount of stress and intensity of the trigger will add more to the cup as they are increased.

If you are the victim of a trauma, your cup will already be partially full. Experiencing trauma has lasting effects which is why the cup is already partly full. This would be your set point.

Healthy coping strategies help to control the amount of stress in your life. These strategies help to empty your cup and as a result, reduce the amount of stress in your life.

Stress is the number one trigger of a bipolar episode.

2. Toxic Relationships
Relationships are complicated. They can build you up or break you down.

Maintain relationships with those people that have a positive influence upon your life. You don't want people in your life that will bring you down and destabilize your bipolar disorder.

It isn't always easy to see the immediate impact a particular individual has upon you. Sometimes, it can take years to realize that a person is a trigger.

Once you find that a person is toxic to your illness, take action to reduce or eliminate this trigger. Eliminating your triggers completely or reducing them will help you manage your bipolar disorder long-term.

3. Death of a Loved One/Bereavement
You would think that the death of a loved one would trigger a depressive episode. However, the death of a loved one and bereavement can actually trigger mania or hypomania. It seems counterintuitive, but that is the reality of this illness. It never follows logic.

Death is never easy, and you cannot control it. Try your best to get the extra support you need and focus on your self-care.

4. Breakup/Divorce
The end of a relationship has been compared to the death of a close loved one. A breakup or divorce (the death of a relationship) can be extremely stressful.

Focus on self-care activities that will improve your ability to cope. Try your best to reduce the fallout from the end of your relationship by utilizing healthy coping techniques.

If you need to add a couple extra workout sessions during the week, do it. Utilize self-care activities that will help center you and recharge your energy stores.

Reach out for support. Talk to your family, friends, and therapist. Your therapist can provide professional suggestions that will help you cope.

Breakup and divorce are both the end of a relationship. They aren't the end of your life but a new beginning.

5. Sleep

Sleep keeps your mind and body functioning at its optimal level. A good night's sleep will recharge you for the following day.

There are certain considerations you need to remember when living with bipolar disorder.

A symptom of a manic (or hypomanic) episode is an increase in energy with little to no need for sleep, yet still feeling refreshed. Your need for less sleep is the result of a manic (or hypomanic) episode.

The opposite can also occur. Having too little sleep can trigger a manic episode. The manic (or hypomanic) episode results from your lack of sleep.

This same line of reasoning can extend to a depressive episode.

A symptom of a depressive episode is a decrease in energy and a need for more sleep. Here, the need for more sleep is a result of the depressive episode.

A depressive episode can be the result of hypersomnia, or too much sleep. Too much sleep can trigger a depressive episode.

Focus on getting at least 8 hours of sleep each night and schedule both your wake and sleep time. This is how you can improve your sleep hygiene.

6. Seasonal Changes

Seasonal changes can be extremely triggering.

Studies suggest those experiencing bipolar depression or unipolar depression have lower levels of Vitamin D. Ask your doctor to check your Vitamin D levels with a quick blood test. To increase your Vitamin D level, you can either take a Vitamin D supplement or get more sunlight.

It gets darker, earlier in the day, when we fall back an hour in the fall for daylight savings. This decreases the amount of available sunlight.

It is no surprise that Vitamin D levels decrease in the fall with less sunlight. As a result, there is a higher incidence of depression during this time of year.

The opposite occurs in the spring and summer time. More sunlight increases a person's level of Vitamin D. Spring and Summer are the times that many people living with bipolar disorder experience manic (or hypomanic) symptoms.

Every person is different, but the change in seasons can potentially trigger a manic (hypomanic in type 2) or depressive episode.

7. Weather Changes

Daily weather changes can directly impact your functionality. Changes in weather are out of your control.

However, you can always take steps to cushion this situation. Focus your attention on your daily treatment plan and amp up your self-care activities.

Prevention is the best approach to the long-term management of your bipolar disorder. Prevention takes time and effort but in the end, you will have more control of your bipolar disorder.

8. Alcohol/Drugs

Many who are undiagnosed with bipolar disorder self-medicate with alcohol and drugs. For the person living with undiagnosed bipolar disorder, self-medicating helps them feel better. Unfortunately, drugs and alcohol make everything worse.

Drug and alcohol abuse destabilizes the person living with bipolar disorder.

Using alcohol and drugs completely negates the positive effects of the medication you are taking. To your body, it's like you didn't take your meds.

Alcohol and drugs are big triggers.

9. Pregnancy

Some expectant mothers experience decompensation through their pregnancy or after their kid is born. In fact, some receive their initial diagnosis of bipolar disorder during or after their pregnancy.

Open communication with your doctor is critical if you are pregnant and managing bipolar disorder with medication. Some medications you can take while pregnant while others you cannot.

Discuss all of your options with your doctor before making a final decision on your treatment.

10. Job Loss

Job loss is a big trigger. The blow can be even more devastating if you've been at the same company for a period of time.

You may also simply be trying to change positions or find another career. If this is your situation, create a barrier against the incoming stress.

To create a barrier against stress, follow your daily treatment plan and spend more time decompressing. This will help you to cope during times of change and added stress.

10. Medication

Never, and I mean never, stop taking medication on your own. Always make changes to your medication regiment under the supervision of your doctor. Please discuss anything related to medication with your doctor. Remember, they are the experts.

Abruptly stopping medication can cause adverse reactions and withdrawal. This in turn, can cause you to destabilize and trigger an episode.

There are different approaches to medication management when it comes to bipolar disorder because there are different types.

For example, I live with bipolar disorder type 1. Stimulants and antidepressants can potentially trigger a manic episode. A mood stabilizer and antipsychotic can create a safeguard in case I need an antidepressant in my cocktail of meds.

When it comes to the topic of medication, speak with your doctor.

11. Financial Strain

Financial stress is an ongoing issue for everyone.

Each person has their own techniques to battle financial strain. For me, having a budget and sticking to it is the best approach for myself and my family.

I try not to purchase anything on credit. If I do, I pay it off the same month. If you don't have the money, don't buy it. Make it that simple.

I never take out extra loans. If I don't have the money, I don't purchase it. Keep away from debt by simply not creating any.

Don't fall for the good debt and bad debt argument.

Many people carry around some amount of debt. If you fall into this category, focus on paying it down.

A friend of mine advised me to live beneath my means. He said to maintain my lifestyle with the support of one income. With the other income stream, save and pay down my debt. Of course, this only applies if you have two sources of income coming in. This is a great piece of advice. If one person loses their job, you will be prepared.

"Always expect the worst, but hope for the best!" There is real wisdom in this statement.

Preparation needs to permeate throughout your management of bipolar disorder and branch into all other areas of your life.

Give any credit cards or debit cards to your partner or loved one if you feel an episode coming on.

Preparation is your best friend in the long-term management of your bipolar disorder.

12. Traumatic Event/Victim of a Crime
Any type of trauma can trigger an episode. In fact, you may have experienced a traumatic event and not even realized it. That happened to me, and I didn't fully comprehend the impact of the situation until a professional pointed it out.

This is an example of why I need the support of experts to help guide me along my journey.

Many times it's apparent when you live through a traumatic event or are the victim of a crime.

In either case, immediately seek out the support of a professional.

13. Too Much Exercise
Over-exercise can potentially trigger a manic episode. Most of the time, this isn't an issue. In fact, I have never experienced this firsthand. Just be aware that this is a possibility.

Last Thoughts
Pinpointing your triggers will help your self-awareness. When you discover your triggers, you discover more about yourself. Your increase in self-awareness will help you in the long-term success of managing your bipolar disorder.

Learning more about yourself and your own bipolar disorder will help to support your long-term goal of stability.

Electronic Device Usage

IN TODAY'S SOCIETY, electronic devices are a necessary evil. I understand your desire to be connected. I am the same way.

Maintain your focus of moderation when it comes to the use of electronic devices. You can easily waste a large portion of your day spending it on social media and other applications.

Give yourself a time limit. Set up a schedule.

When it comes to the recreational use of your electronics, limit your use to certain times throughout the day along with a maximum time limit.

Try to eliminate the use of your electronics to no less an hour before you go to bed. Two hours is even better.

The blue light emitted from the screen of your electronic device throws an "on" switch in your brain. Just like the light coming through your window in the morning triggers your brain to wake up, so does the blue light emanating from your phone, computer, or other electronic device.

If I don't limit the amount of time I spend on my computer or phone, I can easily blow through a couple hours in the blink of an eye.

If you don't monitor your device usage, it can quickly consume your life. Spending too much time on your electronics does not give you the proper amount of time for your other self-care activities.

The idea is to limit your electronic device usage and find a routine that works for you.

Remember, the treatment of bipolar disorder isn't limited to one approach.

Monitoring your electronic usage along with your other self-care activities will positively impact how you manage your bipolar disorder.

Should I Get a Therapy Animal?

IF YOU LOVE ANIMALS, a therapy animal may be exactly what you need. Your doctor can prescribe or suggest you get an animal as part of your treatment plan. Therapy animals have been shown to reduce depressive symptoms and blood pressure in patients.

A dog or a cat can motivate you to get going each day. For example, you have to take your dog outside to go potty. Plus, your cat or dog requires daily water and food.

Taking care of your pet is a great way to build routine in your life and to foster physical activity. They provide a positive reason to get up each day.

If you rent a house or apartment that charges a fee for animals, let them know you have a therapy animal. They will give you some paperwork for your doctor to fill out stating that you require your animal for medical purposes. You cannot be charged extra fees for the medical necessity of a therapy animal.

While traveling, tell whichever pet-friendly hotel you are staying at that you have a therapy animal. They can't charge you extra.

A few years ago, my family and I traveled to the Midwest with my therapy dog. I let the front desk clerk know we had my therapy dog with us. They didn't charge us an extra nightly fee.

Take note that a therapy animal is different compared to a service animal. With a therapy animal, you need your doctor's recommendation and for them to fill out any required paperwork. A service animal is formerly trained to help in some specific way. For example, some service dogs can sense a seizure about to happen in an epileptic patient. Others are Seeing Eye dogs.

It is a big commitment to adopt a pet. You need to take into account the time and expense to take care of your animal's needs.

The daily activities required to take care of your pet will encourage a better routine.

Speak with your doctor to see if a therapy animal is right for you.

Money, Money, Money

MONEY IS ONE OF THE MAIN TOPICS couples argue about. When it comes to money, people have different ideas, views, and perspectives to spend and save.

Bipolar disorder can directly impact your money issues. Spending money frivolously is one of the hallmark diagnostic criteria of bipolar disorder. It is not uncommon for individuals with bipolar disorder to buy 15 iPods, 15 pairs of shoes, or a brand new sports car on a whim.

Before frivolous spending becomes an issue, chat with your partner and make a plan. Remember, taking preventable measures will help you manage your bipolar disorder long-term.

Have your partner take the credit cards, bank cards, and checkbook when you feel the start of an episode. Your partner and other support team members can watch for changes in your mood and behavior. Make sure to note this plan of attack in your treatment plan.

You can have legal documents drawn up to change the power of attorney from yourself to a loved one during an episode.

The document would outline who has authority when the individual with bipolar disorder experiences an episode. During a bipolar episode, this document would take effect. Once a doctor signs off that the patient is no longer in a mood episode, power of authority would switch back.

Again, speak with a lawyer if you have any questions.

When deciding who should take financial responsibility while you are going through an episode, think of who you trust. It doesn't have to be a spouse or partner. You can appoint a parent, a sibling or even a lawyer.

You can reduce financial strain on your life by improving your financial situation. Let's look at some practical ways to cut your expenses and increase your income.

Expenses

Cutting or reducing an expense will free up that money to save or spend elsewhere. Reducing an expense is easier to do than increasing your income.

Ways to cut your expenses:

1) Get Rid of Cable

Cancel your cable subscription.

Next, purchase a Roku or other adapter. With the Roku, or other adapter, you can view Netflix, Hulu, Amazon Prime, or Sling TV These are paid services to watch TV shows, live TV, and watch movies.

Purchase one of these subscription services or more. You can sign up online and most providers go month-to-month. There are no annual contracts for most of the popular options.

2) Pay off Your Credit Cards

If you are able, pay more than the minimum amount due on your credit card each month.

If you have multiple credit cards with balances, find a non-profit organization to consolidate your credit cards and pay a lower monthly payment. Just make sure the company you choose is reputable. Using a consolidation company will reduce the total amount of money you would spend compared to if you paid off each credit card separately.

3) Do Not Buy Name Brand

Buy generic or store brand products. They have the same ingredients as the name brand. They are just cheaper and produced by a different company.

4) Purchase from Second-Hand Stores
Buy your clothes from thrift stores. If you have children, buy their clothes from specialty second-hand kids clothing stores.

5) Budget Billing
You can generally use budget billing to pay for your utility bill. You pay a monthly budgeted amount based on your historic usage. Since utilities fluctuate during the year, this may be a good option. At the end of the year you will pay the difference of how much you owe or are credited. Contact your utility company for more information.

6) Purchase In-Home Workout Equipment
You can save yourself some money by purchasing an in-home workout gym. I bought an adjustable pair of weights, fold up bench, pull-up bar and foam roller for less than a year's membership at the gym. Focus on purchasing the basics and you can get the same intense workout at home as you can at a gym.

Over time, it's more expensive to maintain a yearly gym membership compared to equipping your at-home gym.

If you are looking to save money and maintain your health, this is a great option.

7) Buy in Bulk
In the long run, joining a membership grocery store can save you money. Make sure to do some price comparison before committing.

8) Drink Tap Water
Instead of buying soda or other flavored refreshments, drink from the tap. You can save a considerable amount of money. Plus, you will improve your health by drinking water and avoiding sugary soda.

If switching to water is too difficult, try diffusing your water with fruits and/or vegetables.

9) Eat More Plant-Based Meals
It's more expensive to purchase meat compared to plant-based meals. By reducing or eliminating meat, you will also be supporting an ethical cause to save animals.

These ideas will get you started. Brainstorm and see what you come up with. I am sure you can add more to the list.

Income
You can increase your monthly income by working another job or through investments. Most people do not have enough money to invest and live off the interest.

Side jobs are a great way to increase your monthly income. For example, you can shovel driveways in the winter and mow lawns in the summer. If you have a background in writing or graphic design, you can find freelance websites online to make money.

Last Thought
When it comes to your financial situation, plan and prepare.

How to Get Energized when You Feel Exhausted and Depressed

WHEN YOU ARE EXHAUSTED and depressed, the thought of any kind of movement is overwhelming.

How can you do anything when you can't even get out of bed in the morning?

When I experience a depressive episode, I don't have motivation to do anything. My body is physically exhausted, almost to the point of catatonia.

My body feels sick and exhibits physical symptoms such as headache, nausea, vertigo, stomach ache, and body aches.

My mind lies to me and puts a negative spin on my perspective. Literally, on everything. I call these thoughts *stinkin' thinkin'*.

I find myself constantly asking, "Is there any hope?"

Just like there are ways to manage your bipolar disorder, there are ways to manage bipolar depression and exhaustion. In fact, by utilizing these ideas, you may even feel energized. Experiment with these suggestions, see how you feel and what works best for you.

1. Get Blood Work

Many physical ailments can mimic mental health issues. Blood work can rule out these physical issues and help pinpoint others.

Many medications need regular blood work and monitoring. There is generally a therapeutic range for these medications.

Anything below this therapeutic level is sub- optimal.

Anything above the therapeutic range can be toxic and cause negative side effects.

One time, I tried a medication and presented with various symptoms of bipolar depression. My doctor ordered blood work. He found that the medication slowed down my thyroid and that I could take a thyroid medication to level it out. My other option was to simply try a different medication.

Blood work can rule things out and explain your symptomatology. From there, your doctor will help you choose the appropriate course of treatment.

2. Create a Routine

We have discussed the importance of a routine in managing your bipolar disorder. I cannot overemphasize this approach.

Remember the concept of simplicity. Create a routine that is simple and easy to follow. Making things too complicated will decrease your ability to follow through. Schedule your daily activities at specific times.

Creating a routine will help reduce the guesswork in your schedule. You won't feel as anxious or on edge. This will save your energy for the most important activities in your life.

3. Take a Cat Nap

If you are tired, try a short cat nap. This can re-energize you to tackle the rest of the day.

Make sure it is a short cat nap and you don't sleep for hours. Napping for too long can adversely impact your sleep and nighttime routine.

4. Get Outside

I find substantial benefit if I get outside each day.

The fresh air is invigorating, and the sun feels good on my skin. Sunlight increases your Vitamin D level. If your Vitamin D level is too low, this can be indicative of depression.

If it is too overwhelming to get outside, try sitting on a lounge chair on your porch or similar area. I have a chair on the porch that I use in such a situation.

5. Exercise
Exercise is one of the best natural ways to boost your energy level.

I'm sure by now, you realize the great respect I have for exercise in managing bipolar disorder.

Has your therapist suggested that you exercise when you feel depressed and exhausted?

Each time I feel depressed, tired and exhausted, my therapist pushes me towards physical activity.

One time, I pushed myself to exercise when I felt both physically and mentally exhausted. I described this situation to my therapist. I went on to explain that I felt even more spent after my light workout.

He asked, "Can you imagine how horrible you would have felt if you had not exercised?"

Even if it's a 5 minute walk around the house, something is always better than nothing.

Last Thoughts
I may still be tired after trying one of these suggestions, but they can give me enough energy to cope. Please realize it is okay to feel tired after trying one of these ideas.

Just remember, you'll feel better than if you had not tried anything at all.

Top Careers When You Live With Bipolar Disorder

MANY OF US LIVING WITH bipolar disorder have a hard time in the workforce. Most have had dozens of jobs throughout their career. It is hard to keep a job, let alone start and build a career. The variability of bipolar disorder impacts mood, energy level, motivation and ability to function.

Never fear, my friend, there is hope.

With the right tools and support, a career can become a reality.

The digital age has created a platform from which those of us living with bipolar disorder are able to succeed. If you are trying to find a job or start a career, you are in luck.

Blog

Blogs are a great way to start a career. They generally take time to monetize but require a small initial investment. You really only need to invest in hosting and a web address. Both require a fairly minimal cost.

I like blogs because you have the opportunity to wear a number of different hats. You can utilize photography, writing, videography, or a combination of one or more in your blog. Things never get boring.

Just be aware that there is a learning curve. You can take advantage of Google and YouTube to learn everything you require. If you feel like you need some extra support or help, you can always take an online or in-person class.

A blog is very conducive to making your own schedule. You can roll out of bed wearing your pjs and go straight to your computer. You don't answer to anyone else. If you don't feel like working on your blog at a certain time, just wait until later in the day when you do.

You can also monetize your blog by employing sponsors, affiliate links, advertising, and creating your own products.

Entrepreneur

The entrepreneur route could be a great option for you.

You can start an online ecommerce business through eBay or Amazon. Another option is affiliate marketing. Online opportunities are almost limitless.

A traditional entrepreneur sets up a brick-and-mortar business. The issues I see are following a strict schedule and your total time commitment. A business requires a large number of hours and operates at specific times.

Maintaining a consistent schedule is difficult when you have bipolar disorder. Bipolar affects not only your mood, but your motivation, energy level and activity level. With so much variation, it's hard to follow and keep a work schedule. Getting to your business and following an open-to-close schedule could possibly be problematic.

The number of hours required to start and run a business can be taxing for anybody. You can expect to spend a larger amount of time running your business than at a traditional job. This is harder on someone with bipolar disorder because of the added stress. As I previously mentioned, stress is a big trigger for those of us living with bipolar disorder.

Make sure to take the proper preventative measures if you take the entrepreneur route.

Freelancer

Becoming a freelancer gives you a large amount of control.

Whether you are a writer, artist or other independent professional, freelance is a fantastic option.

You decide how much to charge, who to work with and the type of platform to use. You are in control. This is important when you have an illness that can fluctuate from day-to-day.

Virtual Assistant

A virtual assistant is a type of freelancer. You have the same autonomy as a freelancer and the added control.

Virtual assistants work in almost every area. You can focus on a particular niche and make even more money.

Working as a virtual assistant creates the freedom you require when living with bipolar disorder.

Coach

You have the ability to work with the customers that you choose.

As a coach, you decide the platform to use. You can work online in the digital realm or in-person at a brick-and-mortar setting. This provides you a couple of options.

The biggest obstacle I see being a coach is the consistency. You have to be there for your clients and help maintain a schedule and consistency in their own lives.

This can be extremely difficult when trying to maintain consistency in your own life.

If you're deciding whether to be a coach, give it some serious thought. You definitely don't want to flake out on your clients.

Speaker

Before looking in to being a speaker, make sure you have a period of stability under your belt.

A speaker is a wonderful option to pursue. After all, there is nothing more powerful than to hear the story of a survivor.

As a speaker, you need to maintain a strict and consistent schedule. Being stable affords you this option.

The life of a speaker can be overwhelming if you don't implement the proper coping skills and follow your treatment plan. Just remember to go easy on yourself if you choose this route.

Other Options

Finding a job with flexibility is important.

Repetitive task jobs such as assembly work or data entry are great options.

A job with a quiet environment such as a librarian or greenhouse workers are also great possible choices.

Avoid shift work, on-call jobs or jobs with frequent travel since these are the higher stress jobs.

Should I Tell my Boss I Live With Bipolar Disorder?

There is no simple answer to this question.

An employer cannot fire you or let you go because of your medical diagnosis of bipolar disorder. You are legally protected.

The majority of times, my boss supported me and worked with my needs. One employer helped to rearrange the hours and times of my worked shifts.

My suggestion is not to divulge your illness in an initial interview. Personal experience has taught me to first create a working relationship between my employer and myself.

Make sure you take into account all the possible outcomes before making a final decision. Once you reveal your diagnosis of bipolar disorder to your employer, you can't take it back. The information will be out there.

You need to prepare yourself for any repercussions.

Last Thoughts

Some individuals with bipolar disorder are able to function in the normal corporate world. I've never fit into this traditional corporate role.

Those of us with bipolar disorder generally have a more difficult time navigating a career. Don't get down on yourself.

Having bipolar disorder shifts the paradigm from your so-called healthy self to your ill self. Your "healthy self" is who you were before your diagnosis. Your "ill self" is who you become after your bipolar disorder emerges. You'll find a different road map for each variation of yourself.

The sooner you can grieve the loss of your healthy self and move on, the better off you'll be.

The sooner you can accept both your limitations and strengths, the better off you'll be.

Hobbies

HOBBIES ARE A GREAT WAY to decompress and cope with your bipolar illness. Many of the hobbies I enjoy are written into my own treatment plan as options for coping strategies.

My only piece of advice is to start a new hobby before you experience a depressive episode. It's harder to start anything when you're in the throes of bipolar depression (and mania for that matter).

There are so many hobbies from which to choose. The following are examples that have helped me. Try them and see what you think.

Art
Art encompasses a variety of mediums. Examples include drawing, painting, photography, knitting, music, and scrapbooking.

If one of these artistic examples interests you, visit your local library and checkout a book. You can also look for a class at your nearest community college or take an online class.

I love to draw. I have a number of books that have taught me the fundamentals. Drawing gives me a chance to focus totally and completely on my piece of artwork.

Just because you have bipolar disorder, doesn't mean that you have to be artistic. I have some friends living with bipolar disorder that don't have an artistic bone in their bodies. Just like many others, they never gravitated towards the arts.

There is a strong correlation between creativity and bipolar disorder. However, no causal relationship has been proven.

If you have never expressed your creative ability, give it a shot. You may be surprised.

Watching Movies/Television

As a hobby, watching movies and television are great ways to unwind. They give you the opportunity to decompress and get immersed in another life or world.

Most people watch too much TV If you fall into this category, regulate the amount of time you're watching.

TV and movies are wonderful tools to give our minds some relief. They provide a much needed break from an already chaotic reality fueled by bipolar disorder.

Reading

Reading is such a wonderful hobby and self-care activity. Your imagination is in the driver's seat.

Getting lost in a good book is extremely therapeutic.

There are many reading platforms. You can read a hardback such as a novel or even a comic book or a digital version like an e-book or graphic novel.

There are so many genres from which to choose. Find a topic you'd like to learn more about and start reading.

Last Thoughts

There are countless ideas for hobbies. I suggested a handful that have helped me.

When deciding on a hobby, make sure you enjoy it. The last thing you want to do is make a hobby a chore. It should be a component of your overall treatment plan.

Long-term and Short-term Goals

GOAL SETTING IS IMPORTANT.

When it comes to setting goals, a person living with bipolar disorder is not on equal playing ground as a neurotypical individual.

It is a chemical and biological certainty that the mind of an individual living with bipolar disorder is completely different to that of a person without the illness.

Long-term goals are great if you are a neurotypical individual.

If you live with bipolar disorder, long-term goals can actually be counterproductive and quite discouraging. Short-term goals should be your focus.

Some days, you won't feel like you'll be able to get through it. Any person who has stared mortality in the eyes can relate to this notion.

Many times throughout my life, I've broken up the day into manageable intervals. It has gotten so bad that I've broken down the day into 10-minute intervals just to survive. I remember saying to myself, "I made it through the past 10 minutes, focus on getting through the next 10."

These intervals are my short-term goals. Creating multiple short-term goals throughout the day can save your life.

What if you're not in crisis mode?

Anyone with bipolar disorder can benefit from setting short-term goals. These goals can be for a day, week, or even as long as a month. Personally, I try not to set goals lasting longer than a week.

When I work on projects that last longer than a week, I break that time period up into smaller short-term goals.

It's extremely difficult for me to have any type of realistic long-term goal. They become too overwhelming, and it's easy for me to get discouraged. I know this line of thinking is difficult to understand if you don't live with bipolar disorder.

Short-term goal setting provides greater flexibility than a long-term goal.

With bipolar disorder, there is a high level and degree of uncertainty. Your illness can surface at any time.

Guilt, shame, and other nasty things result from the fallout of an episode.

It is easier to pick up from where you left off if you were working on a specific goal for a one-week period compared to a month or more.

A mood episode can derail you for weeks, months, or even years. Realizing you didn't reach your long-term goal after an episode can be devastating. It can plague you like a parasite to the point you can't function.

When creating goals, be completely transparent and realistic with yourself.

Be skeptical if you hear a so-called "guru" telling you how to live your life. The advice may be acceptable for a neurotypical person but not for those of us living with bipolar disorder.

We are all human, but the mind of a person living with bipolar disorder is completely different to that of a neurotypical individual.

Living with bipolar disorder, we are simply wired differently compared to everybody else.

High Sensitivity and Bipolar Disorder

IT HAS BEEN MY EXPERIENCE that most of us living with bipolar disorder are extremely sensitive to other people's energies, five senses, relationships, and emotions. It seems to be an exception to this rule that a person with bipolar disorder isn't highly sensitive.

Think about your interactions with others and your environment.

Are you sensitive to the actions of others?

Do sounds, images, and feelings overwhelm you?

After you spend time with others, do you feel drained?

Our journey with bipolar disorder opens our lives to struggle and adversity. We need to be more self-aware because it takes work to manage our illness.

Experiencing adversity helps us to create a greater sense of empathy. If you don't deal with adversity in a healthy way, it can create bitterness.

Bitterness arises when you take the victim role. An individual playing the victim will blame others for their struggles and issues. A common trait is not taking personal responsibility.

Fight through adversity and your struggles by empowering yourself. Take personal responsibility for what you are able to control. This builds sympathy for the struggles of others and as a result, increases your sensitivity to everything around and inside you.

Look at this greater sensitivity as a positive trait. It takes a strong, compassionate and caring person to see from another person's perspective.

To actually feel, understand and connect with another human being on such a deep level shows how someone living with bipolar disorder can have a greater sensitivity to others.

Personal Responsibility

IT CAN FEEL LIKE YOU have no control living with bipolar disorder. It is a mental illness that marches to the beat of its own drum.

If you don't have control, how can you be held responsible for your own actions?

Here's the thing, you have more control over your illness than you think.

In a full-blown manic episode, keeping yourself safe and reducing the potential fallout is all you can do. In the middle of an episode, you don't have much control. To take the control back, you need to focus on prevention. Do something before you are in a mood episode.

Prevention is the best approach in reducing the severity of an episode and its length. On a daily basis, follow your treatment plan, work on your self-care, take your medication and keep track of your moods and how you are feeling. To maintain long-term success in your treatment focus on the things you can control.

Keep a mood chart and journal. You can use a mood app, or you can download and print a physical copy of a mood chart. Take a daily inventory of your mood, energy, anxiety, motivation, and other symptoms. Taking this daily inventory will increase your long-term success and self-awareness.

With an app, chart or notebook, track your mood. Journal how you are feeling and what you are doing and going through. It will help you to identify possible triggers, how your illness presents, and your daily functionality.

Taking daily, healthy action will empower you. You will feel more in control and not so powerless.

During an episode, you are in crisis mode. At this point all you can do is survive and receive proper medical treatment. Keeping yourself and others safe is top priority.

For me, my long-term goal is to reduce the severity and length of my episodes.

From the time I was diagnosed with bipolar disorder, compared to today, my bipolar disorder has drastically improved. The length in between episodes is much greater and the severity is much less.

I am a perfect example how bipolar disorder is manageable with the proper treatment, tools, and support.

Dating and Relationships

LIVING WITH BIPOLAR DISORDER adds a new dimension to relationships and the dating scene.

The question is, "Should I divulge my illness to the person I am dating?"

The answer to this particular question is more about listening to your heart than anything else.

Consider some questions:

How long have you been dating?

How long have you known this person?

Do you see yourself in a long-term committed relationship?

Is the relationship serious or just for fun?

There is such a stigma surrounding bipolar disorder. I made sure the person I was with knew me first before divulging my bipolar disorder. I didn't want my potential partner to judge me based on stigma.

There is no rule how long you should be dating before speaking about your illness. You need to do what is right for you and your situation.

Some people I know are very open about their illness, right off the bat, while others take their time to open up about it.

Parenting When You Have Bipolar Disorder

LET'S FACE IT, parenting is difficult. Add bipolar disorder to the equation, and you have a whole new ballgame.

I'm a parent with two kids. I'm not an expert, but I do have personal experience to back up my ideas and claims.

Positive Outcome

We've spoken about the importance of routine and consistency in managing bipolar disorder. These same concepts extend to children. Providing consistency and routine for kids helps them to develop positive coping skills and how to deal with life.

Negative Consequences

If you have kids, you know how impulsive they can be. It takes time for them to learn how to follow directions. Their minds are still developing.

Adults can decide to follow a certain schedule and stick to it. A routine and schedule can be presented to an adult and they simply follow it.

Kids provided with a schedule can be defiant.

As a parent, it is our job to model good behavior.

You teach your kids by explaining the pros and cons of a certain action or decision. Even after explanation, kids may still not understand the potential consequences or outcomes. It takes time for kids to learn the skills that adults so easily take for granted.

Adults and children have different perspectives. Adults have more experience and maturity.

How Having Children Affects a Person with Bipolar Disorder

Kids are a wonderful incentive to stay healthy and follow your treatment plan. They become the reason to stay on this earth and fight the battle against bipolar disorder.

Impulsivity is a hallmark of children. Their newly formed minds just don't have the capacity to think about consequences like adults. An individual experiencing a manic episode has a lack of impulse control similar to kids.

The goal is the same whether you are an individual living with bipolar disorder or a child. This goal is to follow a schedule and maintain consistency during day-to-day living.

Each patient with bipolar disorder is different how they react to a failed routine or inconsistency in their schedule. For some, their stress shoots through the roof with a change. Others can handle it better.

If you have an issue related to your kids, enlist the help of others.

You can't prepare for everything when it comes to your kids. Do your best by putting a plan in place and seek out help if you need it.

Never feel less of a person because you need support. Seeking help proves how strong and self-aware you are to ask for what you need.

Ways to Get the Most Out of Life

LIVING WITH BIPOLAR DISORDER can seem like one big complicated, chaotic mess. It is constant work to manage bipolar disorder.

Is there any time for fun?

How can I be happy living with a mental illness?

There are ways to get the most out of your life living with bipolar disorder.

Focus on the basics and you are already on your way. Remember, keep things simple.

1. Follow Your Treatment Plan

It is imperative that you follow your treatment plan. Fall back on your crisis plan in case of an emergency.

A successful treatment plan will give you energy, help you sleep well, and improve your functionality. If you want stability and to take control of your bipolar disorder, follow your treatment plan.

2. Live a Healthy Lifestyle

Keeping your body and mind healthy will increase your quality of life and help to manage your bipolar disorder. You can do this by adopting healthy lifestyle habits.

Be mindful of what you eat and the amount of exercise you get each day.

If you want to work out at a gym and are a beginner, talk to one of the personal trainers. Generally, they won't charge you to show how to use the machines or aerobic equipment.

If you need some support on healthy eating, try reading a book or hire a registered dietician.

You live in your body from when you are born until the day you die. Treat your body with the respect it deserves.

3. <u>Live Beneath Your Means</u>
Financial hardship causes emotional distress.

Living a frugal lifestyle and beneath your means provides a cushion in case of an emergency. Living from paycheck-to-paycheck is extremely stressful.

Do your best to purchase things that you really need. Focus on your needs and not your wants. If you don't have the money, don't charge it or take out a loan.

The act of saving is actually quite simple. Take money out of your paycheck first thing before you spend it. You can even set up a recurring withdrawal that takes a predetermined amount of money and transfers it into a savings account. Even if you can only start with ten dollars a month, do it. If you are used to making impulsive decisions and purchases, saving money can be a hard habit to start. Saving money now will help you down the road.

If you need to make a major financial decision, take some extra time to think about it. If a third party pressures you to make a snap decision, it probably isn't the right one in the first place.

Living beneath your means will alleviate financial stress and help you to make sound financial decisions for you and your family.

4. <u>Help Others</u>
Helping others is one of the most fulfilling ways you can get the most out of life.

One of the reasons I became a writer is to help others. I love using my experience with bipolar disorder to help others along their own journey. There is nothing better than to get an e-mail or phone call from a person describing how I helped to enrich their life.

If writing is not your thing, volunteer for a cause. There are countless ways to volunteer your time. You can find an organization that fits your beliefs and ideals.

A simple act of kindness, such as smiling or holding a door open for someone, is free and can change a person's day.

By helping others, you will enrich your own life in addition to those around you.

5. Spend Quality Time with Those You Love

Spending time with your loved ones is another wonderful way to get the most out of your life.

Studies indicate the importance of human contact in a person's life.

I remember when I was younger and stayed with my grandparents for about a year or so. Each day, my Nana would tell me, "you know you need at least 14 hugs a day to survive." Her hugs always made me feel better.

If hugging isn't your thing, find something that is.

Go to the park.

Eat dinner as a family.

Hang out with your friends.

Some people don't have the luxury of family nearby. If that is your situation, connect with a phone call.

Sometimes, it is enough to get out among others if you don't have someone special around. You can go to the mall, get a bite to eat by yourself, go to the theater or take a class at your local community college.

Find time to be around others.

6. Find a Hobby

What do you enjoy doing with your free time?

I enjoy drawing and art.

I love to write.

A hike in the Rocky Mountains fills my soul with joy.

Biking with my family is another activity I cherish.

Find something that you like to do. This will ultimately improve your overall quality of life and help lead to personal fulfillment.

Last thought
I hope the suggestions I provided will spark an interest to try something new and to help you find your own way.

Surviving the Holidays

MY FAVORITE TIME OF YEAR is during the holiday season.

For me, the holidays are the embodiment of happiness and joy. It is a time to celebrate family and friends. Whatever your beliefs may be, we can agree we get a chance to focus on compassion, giving and spreading love around.

Many believe the holidays are overly commercialized. There is too little emphasis on the true meaning of the holiday season. The materialistic view of the majority fuels this commercialization.

For many, it is an extremely overwhelming and stressful time of year. The holidays can leave you with a sense of sadness and defeat. Combat these negative feelings by focusing on your treatment plan and your daily self-care activities.

Giving

The holiday season is a great time to help those in need.

Living with bipolar disorder, you need to focus on yourself to manage your illness. There is absolutely nothing wrong with this because you need your health to function and survive.

Self-love is okay. It is not selfish.

It is extremely therapeutic when you are in a state of stability and have the ability to help others. The holiday season provides the perfect opportunity to give to those around you.

Self-care

Self-care is any activity that grounds you and supports your overall health. Another term to describe self-care is coping strategy.

There are both healthy and unhealthy coping strategies.

Examples of a healthy coping strategy are meditation and deep breathing. An unhealthy strategy is binge eating.

Improve your healthy coping strategies and eliminate the unhealthy ones.

We all adopt unhealthy habits at some point in our lives. You may have unknowingly been using an unhealthy coping strategy to manage your bipolar disorder. For example, many individuals self-medicate with drugs and alcohol when living with undiagnosed bipolar disorder.

Speak with your doctor and therapist about your current situation. They can point out any unhealthy coping strategies and advise healthier ways to cope.

Do not have unrealistic expectations. You won't be able to change these habits overnight. It takes consistent practice and effort to eliminate unhealthy habits. Your chances of success will increase if you replace these unhealthy habits with healthy ones.

Your journey to stability will lead to greater enjoyment in your life.

Moderation

I have mentioned the idea of moderation a handful of times. Moderation is one of your best weapons in the daily battle with bipolar disorder.

Control what you can and let go of that which you cannot.

Do not overindulge in anything. Too much of one thing can tip the scales towards a manic or depressive episode.

Moderation takes practice, but it is something you can master.

Bipolar Disorder is an Illness Men Experience Too

MEN GET DIAGNOSED with bipolar disorder just as frequently as women.

Men tend to be diagnosed at a younger age, have more manic episodes and are more prone to a dual diagnosis compared to women.

There is also a societal stigma around how men are supposed to deal with sickness and illness. This stigma developed from earlier generations when men and women had specific gender defined roles.

Stigma is there whether a person chooses to accept it or not. It's the same phenomenon experienced by other social issues. What the surface shows and what is underneath does not always coincide.

As men, we are judged by others when we seek treatment for any type of illness. When I was younger, I struggled with the concept of seeking help. As I have grown older, along with more experience, I no longer let others dictate how I feel.

How can it be a sign of weakness if I take medications and/or go to therapy in an effort to manage my bipolar disorder?

As a man living with bipolar, I need just as much help and support as the next person. In seeking out treatment, I have experienced jokes at my expense, been shunned, yelled at, put down, and minimized.

Men are supposed to be this strong and macho representation of masculinity. We aren't supposed to need any help. We should deal with whatever comes our way. Stigma perpetuates this skewed line of thinking.

Earlier, I spoke about the roles of both men and women in earlier generations. Women were supposed to stay home and raise children, and men were the breadwinners.

Nowadays, there are no separate lines to define the roles for each gender. Sometimes women are the breadwinners and men stay at home with the kids. Roles aren't clearly defined. Roles are based on the necessity of each separate situation. Like other social issues, stigma still lingers regarding gender roles.

It is common for those of us living with bipolar disorder to have multiple jobs over a lifetime. It's difficult to maintain the consistency of a job when you experience a manic or depressive episode.

The expectations of society dictates you should go to college, earn a degree, get a job, and work until you retire. It is easy to feel inadequate if you don't fall in line with these expectations.

It blows my mind how poorly the mentally ill are treated. As a society, we've come a long way but we need to keep moving forward. No one, under any circumstances, should make someone dealing with an illness feel less than a person.

As a man, we are supposed to be these strong pillars that can't be hurt by anything. A mental illness, such as bipolar disorder, should not affect us. Society promotes this ludicrous notion.

A way we can combat stigma is to educate and offer resources for those who need it.

Men need to feel comfortable seeking out help and support. In order to open up, we need to be real, transparent and practice compassion. I've known some men to ask for help, only to be mocked because they aren't "acting like a man" or they should "man up". This isn't a time to make jokes or to make snap judgments.

Just like anybody, men need to be taken seriously and not minimized for receiving treatment for their bipolar disorder. It's hard to ask for something when the other party is mocking, joking and not listening.

What is that Martin Luther King Jr. quote?

"Darkness cannot drive out darkness; only light can do that. Hate cannot drive out hate; only love can do that (passiton.com, 2019)."

Ways to Bounce Back from a Bipolar Episode

DEPRESSION AND MANIA are the two poles of bipolar disorder. They are completely different mood states, but the recuperation time after an episode is similar in both cases.

Bouncing back from a manic or depressive episode is similar to the concept of working out. If you over train, you will eventually experience some sort of injury. This injury can totally derail your progress. You may need to take some time away from your daily workouts.

When a manic or depressive episode hits, this is the injury. It abruptly stops your progress.

It is extremely discouraging when you experience a bipolar episode after you've invested time and effort into managing your illness. Never ever give up hope.

I've noticed an interesting theme in my journey. I've been actively treating my bipolar disorder for 20 years. The fallout, after a bipolar episode, grows less and less with each occurrence. I bounce back from an episode much faster.

I've invested time, energy, money, and my life into managing my illness. My journey proves that you can successfully manage bipolar disorder with the proper treatment.

I've noticed an inverse relationship between the length of my treatment and severity of bipolar disorder. As I spend more time managing my bipolar disorder, the severity of my symptoms decrease and the time between episodes gets greater and greater.

Bouncing back after an episode is similar to muscle memory from working out. Once you resume your workouts after an injury, you will make quicker gains because your body will "remember" adapting to your exercise program.

The same approach relates to the management of bipolar disorder. You will need to slowly build up to where you were before the episode.

Master the daily tasks of living and survival. It's relearning those simple activities needed to survive.

Remember to give yourself time to recuperate. The time to recover from a bipolar mood episode is different for everyone. Don't put unnecessary stress on yourself for not following a timeline or adhering to a specific schedule. Your mind and body both need time to recharge and heal. Allow yourself this time.

After an episode I tend to get easily overwhelmed, so I like to make things easy and simple. Don't make the recovery process any harder than it has to be. It's already hard enough.

Just don't complicate things further if you can control it. Engage in activities that you enjoy and help you to move forward.

This isn't the time to make a big change like moving to a new residence, starting a new job, or ending a relationship.

Keeping the stress to a minimum will decrease your recovery time.

Your response rate, to bounce back from a bipolar episode, will get quicker and quicker as time goes by.

College

HEADING OFF TO COLLEGE is an amazing opportunity. College also brings with it a new set of potential challenges.

It is better to prepare and take a proactive role in getting the most out of your college experience as you can.

When I went off to college in the late '90s, things were different regarding mental health. At the time, I knew nothing about mental illness. Only when I sought out answers did I learn about bipolar disorder.

Luckily, I had the amazing support of the health center on campus. My doctor took the time to educate me, helped me create a treatment plan, and taught me about coping strategies and self-care.

During my college career, I discovered specific ways to manage my new diagnosis of bipolar disorder type 1.

1. Get Involved

Find activities on campus that you can participate.

Join a club. Start your own club. Connecting with others on a more intimate level will provide greater fulfilment in your life at college. This way, you won't feel like just another number at a large university.

Special events take place every day on campus. If you take an active role in your education, you will find there's actually not enough time in the day to take advantage of all the wonderful opportunities. That was my experience. I wanted to take advantage of every single one.

There are countless ways to get involved and participate in campus life.

2. Exercise

Follow a regular exercise program.

Generally, college is the first time most people are away from home and on their own. There's no better time than college to adopt a healthy lifestyle.

I found exercise to be an integral part of my daily self-care. I still do today. At the time, I didn't specifically reference exercise as self-care, but that is the term we presently use.

I maintained a very active lifestyle in college. My main source of transportation was my bicycle. Biking became my mode of transportation to travel to school and work. I also worked out at the gym in the morning and the evening.

Working out in the morning was a great way to get energized and mentally prepare for the day. An evening workout provided a means to destress from the day. More than likely, I was amped up from my bipolar disorder with all the extra energy I had flowing through my body.

As a coping strategy, exercise is a very healthy technique to manage life and maintain balance.

Just make sure your workout routine is realistic and manageable.

3. Sleep

Sleep is a core component to a healthy lifestyle. It helps you to re-energize, build up your immune system, destress and repair both your body and mind.

If you live with bipolar disorder, too little sleep can trigger a manic episode and too much sleep can trigger a depressive episode. To maintain stability, your sleep hygiene needs to be a priority.

Get a minimum of 8 hours of sleep each night.

Go to bed at the same time each night and get up at the same time each morning. Your sleep and wake times need to be realistic and reasonable. Following a healthy sleep schedule will increase your success in managing bipolar disorder.

Do your best to stay away from all-nighters and raging parties. This will only derail your progress and can trigger a mood episode.

I know this is your college experience. Just be smart in your choices.

4. Take Some "Me" Time

College campuses and universities around the world are almost beyond capacity with student enrollment. Students are everywhere, and any alone time is at a premium.

"Me" time needs to be one of your priorities. Find something you enjoy doing where you can be by yourself and with your own thoughts.

Finding "me" time will help you become more comfortable in your own skin and with yourself. It builds self-confidence and gives you the opportunity to deal with your own thoughts and feelings.

Possible activities include meditation, reading, going for a bike ride, drawing, writing, painting, and knitting.

Adopt a hobby and find some time for yourself.

5. Don't Overextend Yourself

Try not to take on too much.

I previously suggested that you should get involved with campus activities as part of your college career. It's a great way to manage your overall health.

Like most things, you need to remember moderation. Balance is key. Too many irons in the fire, and you risk the destabilization of your bipolar disorder.

I have a tendency to take on too much. This tendency followed me as I went off to college.

I eventually learned it is okay to say "no" in order to maintain healthy boundaries. I wish I learned this at a younger age.

<u>Last Thoughts</u>

Whether you live with a mental illness or not, adopt these suggestions to better your college experience.

What Is Success when You Live With Bipolar Disorder?

LIVING WITH BIPOLAR DISORDER is a completely different experience compared to a neurotypical individual. You cannot compare my journey to a neurotypical individual. My mind is wired and operates in a way that you can't understand unless you live with bipolar disorder.

Take care in who you trust and listen to for advice. The only way you can truly understand bipolar disorder is by living with it.

I am in no way minimizing the journey of others. Each person experiences their own hardships.

Don't compare yourself to others. Especially the neurotypical individuals in your life. They are on a different path and journey.

The only comparing you should do is against yourself. Strive to better yourself each day. Some days you will take one step forward and 3 steps back. Don't let this discourage you and halt both your progress and recovery. Simply get up and fight again. Each day is a new beginning.

Bipolar disorder is a daily battle. You will not win every day. However, as time progresses, you will become an expert in the symptomatology of your own bipolar disorder. The number of days you win the battle will slowly increase and the losses will become far and fewer.

It is easy to play the "what if" game. Don't make yourself a participant. Focus on yourself and your own accomplishments. This is extremely difficult to master but well within reason. Try reframing your thoughts and practice this on a consistent basis.

Give yourself credit how far you've come in your own life. You don't need to do x, y, and z to be successful. Live your own journey and truth. There is no particular schedule or timeline you need to follow.

Simply surviving the day is enough. This is success and already makes you successful.

Don't waste your energy on what you can't do or what you do not have. That negative energy will consume you.

Instead, focus on your strengths, what you can do and what you have. Channeling this positive energy will build you up.

Focus on what you can do. Yes, I can survive and get through the day. I can get up and eat breakfast, workout out for 30 minutes, play with my kids, fix lunch, run errands, brush my teeth, take a shower, watch a movie or read a book, draw, paint, knit, carry on a conversation, and whatever else you have the capability to accomplish.

Turning your focus to what you can do will create a positive space in your head. A positive and healthy environment provides a platform from which you can thrive.

Only compare your own journey to itself. I am a different person compared to the individual I knew when I was first diagnosed. The success I have had in my own life has surpassed anything I could ever dream.

To be honest, I never thought I would have made it past my 30th birthday. Here I am, alive and well today. I celebrated my 40th birthday at the end of 2018.

Yes, that is success in my book.

Surviving When Your Partner Has Bipolar Disorder

IF YOU ARE THE PARTNER of an individual living with bipolar disorder, I bet you have experienced many mixed emotions over the course of the relationship with your loved one.

Not only do you have to deal with the normal range of emotions within a normal relationship, but the extreme variability of bipolar disorder. Your journey spreads to encompass the peak intensity of mania to the low ebb of depression.

You use the same strategies to navigate a relationship whether or not you have bipolar. Take action to manage your life and relationship.

There are some basic survival strategies you can implement while in a relationship with a person living with bipolar disorder.

You will see that the suggestions are the same strategies I mentioned for your loved one living with bipolar disorder.

Let's take a look.

Exercise

I am passionate about the use of exercise as a coping strategy.

Exercise is one of the top tools to foster a healthy mind, body and lifestyle. It is an extremely effective coping technique.

Exercise needs to be a priority in your daily life.

You will find improvement in your overall quality of life and ability to function. This is even more important when you are in a relationship with an individual living with bipolar disorder.

Self-care

Make sure you include "me" time in the normal course of a day.

Let's face it, a relationship takes work. Adding bipolar disorder into the equation will increase the stress in your relationship. How you handle this stress will make you or break you.

You can love another person with all your heart, but the fallout from a mood episode can decimate your relationship. Take actionable steps to keep yourself healthy and to function at an optimal level.

"Me" time is taking the time to do something for yourself. Whether you like to read, get a massage, listen to music, take a drive or go for a jog, find the time. The important thing is to spend time with yourself.

This will help you to recharge and cope with your situation.

Open Communication

Honesty goes hand-in-hand with open communication. You cannot maintain open communication if you don't have a foundation of honesty.

Creating an environment that fosters open communication can be difficult. It takes time and hard work.

You can't read your partner's mind. Body language you can interpret, but your best course of action is to always be open and honest.

Create an Action Plan

Keep a written list of your partner's medications and dosages.

Make sure you have the names and numbers of all medical professionals treating your partner. This includes your partner's psychiatrist, therapist, and any other medical professionals.

Have a discussion of what steps to take in case of a manic or depressive episode.

Make sure you have a copy of your loved one's treatment and crisis plan.

It may be beneficial to discuss a Power of Attorney with a lawyer. The internet is a great place to find do-it-yourself paperwork for a Power of Attorney, Living Will, and other tools to protect you and your loved one.

Last Thoughts

These are some basic and essential ways to increase the quality of your relationship.

Living with bipolar disorder does not excuse your loved one from harmful behavior. It provides a specific reason as to why.

Do not enable negative and destructive behavior.

Ask your partner what they need. Tell your partner what you need as well.

Work with your partner to take positive steps and action in the management of their illness. Together, create a healthy lifestyle.

With dedication, your relationship can thrive and so can you.

Final Thoughts

BIPOLAR DISORDER WILL ALWAYS BE THERE. It will be your constant roommate for the rest of your life.

You have the opportunity to make the most out of your life with the proper treatment. It takes daily positive action, discipline, and persistence.

If you are newly diagnosed, here is a quick recap of the steps to take after you are diagnosed:

- Acceptance of your diagnosis
- Create a Treatment Plan and Crisis Plan
- Take your medication
- Participate in therapy
- Follow a healthy lifestyle (exercise and good food choices)
- Keep a mood journal to chart your mood, energy level, triggers, and feelings
- Find daily self-care activities to enhance your quality of life
- Take an active role in your treatment
- Advocate for yourself
- Find a hobby
- Spend quality time with those you love

If this seems too overwhelming, take it one step at a time.

Start with creating your treatment plan and crisis plan with the help of your doctor and loved ones. Follow your plan on a daily basis.

Make the treatment and management of bipolar disorder a top priority in your life. Without stability and proper treatment, bipolar disorder will consume you and take over.

If you do not adequately treat your bipolar disorder, it will get worse. The severity and length in time of an episode will increase. This isn't a statement of absolution. There are exceptions to every rule, but this is the common result of not treating bipolar disorder.

The journey to stability can be overwhelming, but don't give up hope. Give yourself enough time to adapt and learn about bipolar disorder.

It is within your reach and ability to successfully manage bipolar disorder. Taking a proactive role in the management of your illness will empower you. This, in turn, will give your more control of your actions and emotions.

Bipolar disorder is like a wild beast. The ability to tame a wild beast is feasible. You just need to take the appropriate steps.

Never give up.

Never give in.

Keep going!

You are a warrior in the daily fight of *The Bipolar Battle*.

You are a bipolar warrior.

Works Cited

AFSP. (2019). *American Foundation for Suicide Prevention*. Online: https://afsp.org/ [Accessed 4 Oct. 2019].

Diagnostic and statistical manual of mental disorders. (2017). Arlington, VA: American Psychiatric Association

Eveningpsychiatrist.com. (2019). *DSM IV Diagnostic Criteria - Bipolar Disorder | Atlanta Psychiatrist Dr. Hege*. Online: https://www.eveningpsychiatrist.com/bipolar/dsm/ [Accessed 6 Oct. 2019].

Healthline. (2019). *Diagnosis Guide for Bipolar Disorder*. Online: https://www.healthline.com/health/bipolar-disorder/bipolar-diagnosis-guide#mental-health-evaluation [Accessed 6 Oct. 2019].

Lexico Dictionaries | English. (2019). *Delusion | Definition of Delusion by Lexico*. Online: https://www.lexico.com/en/definition/delusion [Accessed 6 Oct. 2019].

Lexico Dictionaries | English. (2019). *Hallucination | Definition of Hallucination by Lexico*. Online: https://www.lexico.com/en/definition/hallucination [Accessed 6 Oct. 2019].

Lexico Dictionaries | English. (2019). *Psychosis | Definition of Psychosis by Lexico*. Online: https://www.lexico.com/en/definition/psychosis [Accessed 6 Oct. 2019].

Lexico Dictionaries | English. (2019). *Stigma | Definition of Stigma by Lexico*. Online: https://www.lexico.com/en/definition/stigma [Accessed 6 Oct. 2019].

Lexico Dictionaries | English. (2019). *Trigger | Definition of Trigger by Lexico*. Online: https://www.lexico.com/en/definition/trigger [Accessed 6 Oct. 2019].

Nimh.nih.gov. (2019). *NIMH » Bipolar Disorder*. Online: https://www.nimh.nih.gov/health/statistics/bipolar-disorder.shtml [Accessed 4 Oct. 2019].

passiton.com. (2019). *"Darkness cannot drive out darkness; only light can do that. Hate cannot drive out hate; only love can do that."* Online: https://www.passiton.com/inspirational-quotes/7171-darkness-cannot-drive-out-darkness-only-light [Accessed 7 Oct. 2019].

Study.com. (2019). *What Is Personal Identity? - Definition, Philosophy & Development - Video & Lesson Transcript | Study.com*. Online: https://study.com/academy/lesson/what-is-personal-identity-definition-philosophy-development.html [Accessed 7 Oct. 2019].

TheFreeDictionary.com. (2019). *warrior*. Online: https://www.thefreedictionary.com/warrior [Accessed 6 Oct. 2019].